Holy Living

Worship

Matthew E. Johnson

Elaine A. Heath
General Editor

HOLY LIVING: WORSHIP

ISBN 9781501877582

Manufactured in the United States of America

19 20 21 22 23 24 25 26 27 28—10 9 8 7 6 5 4 3 2 1

ABINGDON PRESS
Nashville

TABLE OF CONTENTS

Foreword 5

Introduction 7

Broadening Worship 11

How Worship Forms Us 41

Worship and Revealing
God's Kingdom in the World 69

Worship in Unexpected Places 99

FOREWORD

From the time that individuals began responding to Jesus' call to follow him, they began to learn rhythms of life that would be essential for them to be able to live their lives wholeheartedly for God. Chief among these practices was prayer. Jesus modeled for them how to withdraw from busy service to spend time alone in prayer. He offered prayer verbally in front of them, and when they asked, taught them to pray with the prayer we now call the Lord's Prayer. Following Jesus' ascension, as the disciples waited in Jerusalem "for what the Father had promised," that is, the Holy Spirit, Luke tells us that "all were united in their devotion to prayer" (Acts 1:4, 14). Prayer was foundational and formational, positioning them to receive the Holy Spirit, God's empowering presence that both indwelled and propelled them.

Following that transformative event, in due time they followed the Spirit's leading and bore witness to Jesus "to the end of the earth" (Acts 1:8). Their lives were busy, on the move, teaching, preaching, healing, explaining, encouraging, and confronting the evil and injustice of their society. Yet all of that doing, they knew, had to emanate from a deeply grounded experience of being. Nurturing a loving relationship with God was a central commitment that they, like we, had to learn to practice. Apart from this relationship, their busyness was meaningless. So they and those who followed them in the faith added to the practice of prayer a wide range of spiritual disciples to strengthen their relationship with God, help them grow in Christlikeness, and fuel them for the work God called them to do.

Some of these practices—things like meditation, simplicity, and fasting—are more inwardly focused. Others are expressed outwardly and corporately—things like confession, worship, and celebration. And some of the practices can be both, such as prayer. All of them—and there are many—work together to help us achieve lives of balance, anchored securely to Christ and equipped for meaningful engagement with others.

This book is one in a series of eight, each of which focuses on a single discipline. In this volume, Matt Johnson challenges us to open our hearts and minds more fully to worship that changes us, forming us more completely into people who love and serve God. I invite you to new understandings and practices of worship.

—Elaine A. Heath, General Editor

INTRODUCTION
Holy Living: Worship

by Matthew Eron Johnson

In my own journey of living as a disciple of Jesus, spiritual practices have been essential. I have read and taught about the spiritual practices since I first began working in a church almost two decades ago. Even with my experience, the spiritual practices are a daunting subject. And worship is so central to the Christian tradition that it seems too big for a little book.

So, instead of being an exhaustive, academic exploration of worship, this book is an exploration of the elements of worship that have been most formative to me and to those who have shared the spiritual journey with me. The book aims to deepen our understanding of worship so that we can worship more fully. Because of this approach, what began as an overwhelming topic quickly became a space where I could personally draw closer to God.

Chapter 1 is dedicated to defining *worship*. To define it gives us clarity and richness. Along with defining *worship*, we explore the concept of a Godward life. This is a life of turning toward God for guidance moment by moment and day by day. Such a life is fuel for genuine worship.

Chapter 2 focuses on the way worship shapes us. Here I draw upon my understanding of Christian spiritual formation in general and how the spiritual practices fit into that formation. Then we look at the specific impact of worship.

Chapter 3 links our formation as disciples of Jesus with Jesus' primary focus, which was the kingdom of God. As we are being formed into Christlikeness, we point to God's action in the world, and we grow in desiring what God desires.

Chapter 4 then allows us to play with the idea that worship can happen in unexpected places. As worship breaks out, our life becomes an increasingly joyful walk with God. My goal is for you to feel excited about practicing worship after reading this book.

Throughout the book, I offer "Active Applications." They are suggestions of steps you can take in regard to a point that has just been made. I have included several Active Applications throughout the book, and it is not my intention for you to do all of them. In fact, attempting to do all of them could be an unhelpful burden. Instead, note the Active Applications that pique your interest, and then return to them when you have finished the chapter.

BLESSING

I live in Wichita, Kansas, which is also home to an amazing Christian bookstore called Eighth Day Books. I told the owner, Warren Farha, that I had written a book on worship. He pondered for just a moment and then said, "Well, Matthew, there is no topic of more significance. Gratitude is at the core of what it means to be human."

As I considered what Warren said, I remembered how much I have enjoyed writing this book: the research, the Scripture, the quotes, the stories, and the connections. I felt as if God was meeting me every day as I wrote. My hope for anyone who reads this book is that they will feel the same way. May you discover the worshipful life!

CHAPTER ONE
Broadening Worship

Many of us need a new, broader, and deeper understanding of worship. We have grown up with, or grown accustomed to, worship as a task on our to-do list. We have limited worship to a weekly gathering of Christians. But what if our understanding of worship is really just a shell of what worship could be?

I have found that my understanding of worship has grown broader and deeper as I have lived a life of following Christ. Like other things in life, I had worship in a box, and that box was too small. Breaking down those boxes can be a powerful experience. I had a similar experience with jazz, and that parallel helped me see the invitation that God is extending to us in terms of worship.

I grew up in rural Indiana and attended a small high school of roughly two hundred students. Although we were small, we did have a music program and even a jazz band, and I played trombone in the jazz band. I learned to read jazz charts, and I learned to mimic the swing of great jazz musicians that I listened to in recordings. It was fun. It was the highest quality our little band could produce. But none of us knew that we lacked the spirit of jazz.

Many years later, I led a team from my church in Kansas down to New Orleans to help with rebuilding after Hurricane Katrina. One man whom our team helped was a professional musician. In fact, he was a trombone player who had toured with Harry Connick Jr. At the end of our first week, he invited us to hear him play at a club called Tipitina's. My team was exhausted from the week of hard work, but we didn't want to miss this opportunity to eat great food and hear great music.

Tipitina's is a large, two-story dance hall with one stage and few seats. You come to dance. And that night, the place was packed. The musicians gathered on stage and began to play. And for the first time, I experienced the spirit of jazz. Oh, I had heard jazz, certainly. I had listened for hours to recordings of Louis Armstrong, Duke Ellington, Ella Fitzgerald, and others. But I had never experienced anything like this. It wasn't just the music, it was the entire atmosphere.

The musicians began with a song, giving us the melody. The crowd responded by immediately moving to the music (not something that ever happened at my high school jazz band concerts). After playing through the melody, the band grew quieter as the trumpet player stepped forward and improvised a solo that hinted at the melody. As the solo grew, I noticed that the trombone player walked over to the clarinet player and improvised a simple background part. It was short and repetitive.

The clarinet player listened for a few bars and then contributed something to what the trombone player had offered. All the while, the solo continued to grow in volume and complexity, and the bass and the drums were keeping it all together and also building with intensity.

Eventually, the saxophone joined the trombone and the clarinet with more harmony. As all of this unfolded, the crowd hung on every note, moving to the music. The soloist, the rest of the band, and the crowd (who would shout out from time to time), were all listening to one another and feeding off one another's energy. The music and the room kept building with anticipation.

Finally, the entire ensemble returned to the central melody of the piece, at full volume. The crowd went wild, yelling and dancing in full motion. Then the band grew quiet again. This time, the clarinet took the solo; and the whole process started again, built again, and released again. It was a powerful interaction of music, musician, and crowd. I had finally witnessed the spirit of jazz.

What if our life of discipleship with Jesus, living in relationship with the Trinity, is meant to be more like this jazz experience at Tipitina's? How many of us are still worshipping as if we are middle school jazz musicians? What if the worshipping we've been doing is only a shadow of the experience that worship can be?

What if worship was an interactive and synergistic experience that happened in planned and unplanned moments of life? What if worship was the result of our relationship with God that shaped the way we interact with others and our community?

WORSHIP, JAZZ, AND THE SONG OF GOD'S LOVE

I have found in my experience of jazz music an analogy for the way we worship. The title of the song we are playing is "God's Grace"! The melody of the song is a fixed thing. It doesn't change. The melody symbolizes organized worship. It is structured and gives a framework for our community's gathered time of worship.

Now, if we stopped here, it wouldn't have to be jazz. It could be a hymn or any other song—a fixed thing that starts and stops. But worship doesn't stop at the end of the worship hour. The song goes on after we leave our church service. When we step out into the world, we enter into the role of the backup musicians. God is the soloist, playing a tune. Our responsibility is to keep listening for that solo and to complement what God is doing with our lives and our words.

As we complement God's solo with our background parts, we find others who are playing backup for God as well. They are people who are responding to God's song of grace. As we join one another in offering backup to God, community begins to form and we are not alone. Instead, we are with a band of others. We find energy and joy in our work together, and we shape the world around us.

While all this is happening, there is a crowd listening. The crowd is the world—our coworkers, our neighbors, our friends, our family members, our enemies. Many of them are waiting for a melody that will make sense of the cacophony of life. They are attracted to the song of God's grace, joy, and abundance. They are curious to meet people who will actually play along with that song rather than playing along with the song of isolation, despair, hatred, scarcity, and shame. When they start to hear the song of God's grace, they can't help but to move, dance, and call out for more.

And all of these interactions can feed and fuel one another, building in intensity until we return to the original melody, which is organized worship. We return to our weekly gathering with new energy and life. And there we hear again the melody, but now we are more energized because we are bringing with us all that we have heard and seen and felt while we were out in the world. We must shout about what God has done, or else the stones will do it for us!

Worship is so much more than we often allow it to be.

DEFINING WORSHIP

From the analogy of a jazz band playing for a crowd, I want to emphasize that worship is dynamic and highly interactive. At its core, worship is built on our interaction with God and what God is doing in our lives. This dynamic, interactive experience we call worship can be simply defined in this way:

Worship is the spiritual practice of responding to God's grace.

While it is simple, it is also expansive and rich with significance. Let's look more closely at a few words in this definition to appreciate what it is offering us.

Responding

The definition of worship is wide-ranging because we can respond to God in so many and such various ways. We can respond with awe, praise, prayer, gratitude, contrition, glorification, celebration, petition, confession, singing, reading, exhortation, and communion, just to name a few.

There are as many ways to worship as there are ways for the heart to express itself to God. This is not a point to be overlooked. We must break down the walls we have placed around worship so that it might surface at any moment in our lives.

. . . to God's Grace

If worship is the spiritual practice of responding to God's grace, then the assumption is that God's grace is present. God's grace is present to us as unmerited forgiveness as well as action in our lives and our world.

Worship does not begin with us, but instead begins with God's action and results in our response. While we may agree conceptually with the idea that God is active in our lives and in our world, seeing God's activity on a practical level can be challenging because we aren't sure what it looks like. Graciously, Jesus revealed God's action in a tangible and beautiful way.

Jesus, as the Incarnation of God, allows us to witness what God desires and see how God acts in the world. Therefore, everything Jesus does helps us understand how God is acting in our lives and the world today. Jesus reveals a God who loves humanity. Because of that love, God is committed to taking any action required to be in relationship with us and cares enough about us to seek our healing, liberation, and formation. And our healing, liberation, and formation are the result of Jesus' tangible actions. Let's just spell out some of them:

- Jesus welcomed people who had been excluded
- Jesus listened to the voiceless
- Jesus healed the hurting
- Jesus forgave sinners
- Jesus guided seekers
- Jesus fed the hungry
- Jesus challenged those who held on to power

There is nothing surprising or radical about this list. But it is easy to miss two important keys. First, every sentence involves Jesus' action. Every verb in those sentences is describing God's action. *Welcomed*, *listened*, *healed*, *forgave*, *guided*, *fed*, and *challenged* are words for what Jesus did.

And the second important key is that the Spirit of Christ is still seeking to do those things in our lives today. So I would encourage you to consider where you are on this list:

- Jesus desires to welcome you
- Jesus longs to listen to you
- Jesus wants to heal you
- Jesus fully forgives you
- Jesus gladly guides you
- Jesus yearns to feed you
- Jesus lovingly challenges you

We can take hold of these actions, allowing them to sink into our hearts, minds, souls, and bodies. In our own lives, when the stranger is welcomed, we are witnessing God's grace at work. When people listen deeply to one another, we are seeing God at work. When we experience restoration, it is God moving in our lives. When we are embraced by forgiveness, it is God's action in our hearts.

When we discover wisdom for how we are to live, this is God's love at work. When we find abundance in a place known for scarcity, it is God's kingdom breaking into our world. When we find our own beliefs and barriers and false narratives being challenged, we are bumping into God's truth. And when our wounded souls become the cavern in which the song of God's love joyously echoes, we are worshipping.

A Spiritual Practice

Finally, our definition for *worship* points out that it is a spiritual practice. This phrase is popular now, but with popularity comes ambiguity, so let's be clear about it. To begin with, the practice itself is not spiritual—you are! What makes any activity spiritual is when you do it with your "heart and mind" set on Christ (Colossians 3). By doing spiritual practices, we are not becoming more spiritual, but we are becoming more aware of our spirituality.

The spiritual practices are practices because they are something we can choose to do. Practice means we don't always do it well, but we can keep practicing at it. And it means it shapes our souls.

The goal is not to practice the spiritual practices; the goal is to be transformed in Christ. Taking on spiritual practices is one way of opening ourselves to transformation. For it is through the spiritual practices that the Holy Spirit can help transform the way we see God, ourselves, our neighbors, and our world.

With time, we come to see all of these things the same way Christ sees them, and therefore it becomes increasingly possible to live our lives in a way that is parallel to the life of Jesus as we see it in the Gospels. This means we can speak the truth in love, engage in conflict, bring healing, love our enemies, live without a need to be noticed for our righteousness, and give our lives for others.

PUNY WORSHIP

When we have a clearer understanding of what worship is, it shines a light on the shadowy half-truths we often believe about worship, and this is valuable. Of all the spiritual practices, worship may be the most familiar and therefore the most overlooked.

Many Christians (myself included) began attending weekly worship before we could walk. Because of this great familiarity, we need to look more closely at our ideas about worship and flesh out possible gaps. When our understanding of worship has false understandings or half-truths, it leads to a puny understanding of worship that can actually be harmful to our souls and to our community of faith. What are some of these half-truths and false beliefs that affect our understanding of worship?

Half-truth: Worship and Church Are Synonyms

First, we can find a more robust understanding of worship by looking more closely at the words *worship* and *church*. For most of the American Christians I have known, *worship* and *church* are used interchangeably. This is acceptable enough as a shorthand, but we need to be intentional and periodically clarify that both of these words mean much more.

While we certainly do go to the church building during the week for community worship, we are missing out if we think church is just a building. A church is a group of two or three people gathered in Jesus' name. This is a fact worth savoring.

When we meet with a friend to share our struggles and to seek God's guidance—we are being church. When we travel with a group of friends to a place where disaster has struck, and we help rebuild to express God's care—we are being church.

When we attend a meeting with others in order to make decisions about the care and function of the church building—we are being church. And when we sit with one or two other people in someone's living room to sing a song, share a meal, and offer our lives to God—we are being church, and we are worshipping corporately.

Half-truth: Worship Is Specifically Communal

More often than we realize, we are being the church, and sometimes those gatherings are worship. But this leads us to our second half-truth. This half-truth states, "Worship is something that can only be done with others." As I've named above, we can and do worship with others, but if this is the only way we consider worship, we are missing out. The rest of the truth is that we can worship in many ways and in many places, including alone.

Richard Foster offers this insightful teaching as he explores steps into worship. "Have many different experiences of worship. Worship God when you are alone. Have home groups not just for Bible study, but for the very experience of worship itself. Gather little groups of two and three and learn to offer up a sacrifice of praise. Many things can happen in smaller gatherings that, just by sheer size, cannot happen in the larger experience. All of these little experiences of worship will empower and impact the larger Sunday gatherings."[1] What an amazing insight!

For over two decades, my wife, Catherine, and I have spent time each morning doing a morning devotion. It has changed and evolved from simply reading Scripture and praying for others, to using a common prayer book, to including Taizé music. But it wasn't until I read the quote above from Richard Foster that I realized this daily practice helped us to be more prepared each Sunday when we showed up for congregational worship.

In the next chapters, we will explore how such a daily practice also helps us prepare for the world we inhabit.

Active Application

Take notice of the ways you use the words worship *and* church. *Do not judge yourself for the way you use these words. What does your use of these terms teach or show you?*

Half-truth: Worship Is a Performance, and I Am the Audience

If you are like me, you know how tempting it is to sit in worship on Sunday morning, feeling as if you are there to be entertained, engaged, and educated. The performers are up front to entertain and to educate us, the audience. When we enter worship with this attitude, we often leave disappointed by various aspects of the service: the preacher seemed unprepared, the accompanist played our favorite hymn too fast, the soloist was off-key, the computer person couldn't advance the slides fast enough to keep up with the reading, and on and on.

And, if you are like me, you also have a deep sense that worship is more than a performance and more than being entertained. In fact, can we really say that "Worship is a performance, and I am the audience" is a half-truth, or is it completely wrong?

I would suggest that there is in fact truth to the statement, "Worship is a performance, and we are the audience." When worship involves more than one person, someone has to lead. And often that person needs to prepare in some way, whether it is selecting the songs that will be sung, preparing a sermon, practicing an instrument, or preparing the slides. And when they share what they have prepared, it is a performance.

And as for the congregants as an audience, there is also an element of truth here. The word *audience* actually has roots in the Latin word *audire*, which means "hear."[2] An audience is a group that hears and grasps what is shared. In this sense, we can say Christians who have gathered together for worship are listening to what is shared.

Things go awry, however, when we allow ourselves to be the endpoint of the performance. Instead of being the endpoint, we are invited to receive the performance and then lift it up and pass it on to God with our own thanks and praise. In many ways, this is easier when the performance is amazing.

I have been at secular concerts listening to professional musicians and felt close to God and moved to a place of gratitude toward God, this in spite of the fact that the performance was in no way framed as a worship service. Through the power of their abilities, the artist turned me toward a God who creates beauty, reveals truth, and fosters goodness.

But what about the moments in worship when the performer is not that good? Here is when our presence as an audience must be more like the crowd at the jazz club I described at the beginning of the chapter.

We have the opportunity to call forth the best in the person who is leading by first surrounding them with prayer, then receiving their offering through attentive listening. And then, in whatever way is appropriate for our congregation, we lift up what is being offered to God. This could be as subtle as leaning forward and nodding our head in affirmation of their offering, or it could include lifting our hands in praise or shouting, "Amen!" Whatever the case, we join our worship with the leader's worship and place it before the Trinity, who delights in the messy artwork of their beloved children.

Active Application

Notice if there are any "messy" parts of worship that annoy you. Can you offer these elements mercy and forgiveness? If so, how does it change your experience of worship?

Fully False: Worship Has to Have [Fill in the Blank]

What elements of worship do you consider "essential"—hymns, choruses, a sermon, an organ, a guitar, a choir, a bulletin, a projector, an offering? Are these elements what make a worship service?

There are two aspects to this statement we need to briefly identify. The first is the human tendency to decide that our favorite part of worship is the essential part of worship; and therefore if worship doesn't include that, it's not real worship. Because the goal of this book is to broaden and deepen our understanding of worship so it leads to a life lived in service to God, we need to address this.

I find the reason many people are attached to specific elements of worship is because they have lived through a church debate about contemporary versus traditional worship. Rather than being a discerning conversation where the Spirit was given space to lead, it turned into a political rodeo, with sides being chosen and winners and losers being identified.

While this is not a universal occurrence, it is sadly not uncommon either. And if you are a person who has been hurt by one of these events, I want you to know your pain, frustration, and disappointment are real. I don't want to glaze over them lightly.

When we discuss worship, we need to be aware of this possible wound. We need to acknowledge the pain that some people carry around this topic. The goal here of bringing up this possible wound is simply to become aware of it. If we don't, the pain of a past decision or argument may be lurking in the background and impacting the way you worship.

Whether you are worshipping with the congregation or worshipping alone, pain or resentment may be shaping your worship. It may be freeing to simply name this and allow it to be part of the conversation as you move through the topics of this book.

There is a second reason I have listed this "false" statement here. Worship is much more than just the components of instruments, projectors, and carpet. When a congregation of people come together to worship God, their worship will include some or even all of the elements I have listed above, plus others. However, it is not those pieces that make worship true worship. Worship happens in many settings and in many ways. It includes, but is not limited to, congregational worship with the elements I have listed above.

Active Application

Create a list of elements that you feel are "essential" to worship. Why do you include these components on your list?

Fully False: Worship Is Something I Do to Get God to Like Me or to Earn God's Favor/Salvation

Any conversation about spiritual practices needs to address this lie. Many people struggle to understand how spiritual practices fit into our lives. Many of us have grown up being warned that we cannot earn salvation from God, which is a great warning to keep in mind. We cannot earn salvation.

But this produces a question: If salvation cannot be earned, then why should anyone do the spiritual practices? The way we answer this question and undo the false statement above is by understanding what spiritual practices actually do and how worship fits into the category of spiritual practice.

First of all, God loves you—period. Full stop. God loved you before you deserved it ("But God shows his love for us, because while we were still sinners Christ died for us" [Romans 5:8]), and God loves you now. You have been given this love as a gift, whether you receive it and enjoy it or not.

You also can't do anything to break God's love. Even if you reject God in every imaginable way, God's love for you will remain. Just as the father of the prodigal son was always watching for the possible return of the younger son (Luke 15:20), so, too, God's love will always be watching for the possible return of anyone who has rejected God.

So, in other words, there is nothing to be earned. However, there is much to be experienced. There are many ways we could name what it is we can experience. We can experience God's love, we can experience life in the kingdom of God, and we can experience God's grace.

The Book of Discipline defines grace as "the undeserved, unmerited, and loving action of God in human existence through the ever-present Holy Spirit."[3] Through spiritual practices such as worship, we intentionally seek God out with a desire to experience God's action in the world and also to collaborate with God's action in the world.

Don't let this get too abstract in your mind. Through Christ, we have been invited to experience a relationship with the God who is love. This means we can move through each moment of each day in companionship with God. Through the ever-present Spirit, we can seek God's wisdom as we make decisions, we can seek Christ's creativity as we face challenges, we can seek the Spirit's comfort as we face insecurity. It is an entirely different way to move through life. And we know what it looks like because that is how Jesus moved through life, as we see in the Gospels.

By grace, we experience God's love at various moments and in various ways. Sometimes it comes in small ways, such as a moment of joy as we watch the sunrise. At other times, it can be a major turning point, as when we hit rock-bottom because of an addiction.

And in the Christian tradition, we have practices that place us before God so that God might work in and through us. Worship is one such practice. When we worship God, we are not earning favor, but we are placing ourselves in a position to be in relationship with God.

Active Application

What have you been taught about spiritual practices and grace? Do you hold spiritual practices at a distance for fear of violating God's grace? Do you engage in spiritual practices like a superstitious activity, hoping God will give you what you want if you do them?

HEARING GOD'S SONG OF GRACE

Now that we've defined *worship* and dispelled a few false ideas about worship, let's look at stories that illustrate what we have named. The Bible gives us many stories of people practicing worship. God moved in their lives in a powerful way, and naturally they responded with praise and thanks. Let's look closely at two stories from the Bible and see what we can learn.

Jacob's Ladder: Stairway to Heaven

Genesis 27 shows a dysfunctional family on full display. It tells us the story of how Isaac's wife, Rebekah, coached the younger son, Jacob, to steal the blessing of the elder son, Esau, by lying to Isaac and pretending to be Esau. When Esau found out the blessing had been stolen, he was so enraged that the only way he could console himself was to ponder how he would kill Jacob.

The only thing keeping Jacob alive was that Esau was going to wait until their father, Isaac, had died; then he would kill Jacob. In an effort to keep Jacob alive, Rebekah made up a reason that he should leave: he needed to find a wife. Rebekah went to Isaac and explained that the local women were intolerable for her and that Jacob should find a wife in the land Rebekah came from. Isaac obliged and sent Jacob to Rebekah's brother, Laban. It is in the midst of this messy story that we read:

> Jacob left Beer-sheba and set out for Haran. He reached a certain place and spent the night there. When the sun had set, he took one of the stones at that place and put it near his head. Then he lay down there. He dreamed and saw a raised staircase, its foundation on earth and its top touching the sky, and God's messengers were ascending and descending on it. Suddenly the LORD was standing on it and saying, "I am the LORD, the God of your father Abraham and the God of Isaac. I will give you and your descendants the land on which you are lying. Your descendants will become like the dust of the earth; you will spread out to the west, east, north, and south. Every family of earth will be blessed because of you and your descendants. I am with you now, I will protect you everywhere you go, and I will bring you back to this land. I will not leave you until I have

> done everything that I have promised you." When Jacob woke from his sleep, he thought to himself, The LORD is definitely in this place, but I didn't know it. He was terrified and thought, This sacred place is awesome. It's none other than God's house and the entrance to heaven. After Jacob got up early in the morning, he took the stone that he had put near his head, set it up as a sacred pillar, and poured oil on the top of it. He named that sacred place Bethel, though Luz was the city's original name. (Genesis 28:10-19)

In this one story, we can see so many important truths illustrated. First, we see grace at work. Jacob had not done anything to deserve the promise God was speaking into his life. Jacob wasn't religious or devout. Up to this point, what we've seen of Jacob is that he was primarily concerned with himself.

We also see that God is active. It was God at work in Jacob's world, with angels ascending and descending on the ladder to heaven. God also made an action-packed promise to Jacob. God said, "I will *give* you . . . [this] land," "I am *with you* now, I will *protect* you everywhere you go, and I will *bring you back* to this land. I will *not leave you* until I have *done* **everything that I** have *promised* you" (verses 13, 15, bold and italics added).

Jacob awakened with worship on his lips. He marveled at the place where he had laid his head and engaged in worship by turning his pillow into a pillar and blessing it with oil as a marker of what God had done. So, on a basic level, we see that this story illustrates what worship is: God acted, Jacob responded.

The Woman of Great Love

We also see worship enacted in the New Testament, especially around forgiveness. Jesus embodied God's gracious forgiveness in a way that deeply touched people. And perhaps no story illustrates forgiveness and worship more powerfully than the story of a woman who showed up at Simon the Pharisee's house to express her deep gratitude to Jesus. The story occurs in Luke 7:36-50.

> One of the Pharisees invited Jesus to eat with him. After he entered the Pharisee's home, he took his place at the table. Meanwhile, a woman from the city, a sinner, discovered that Jesus was dining in the Pharisee's house. She brought perfumed oil in a vase made of alabaster. Standing behind him at his feet and crying, she began to wet his feet with her tears. She wiped them with her hair, kissed them, and poured the oil on them. When the Pharisee who had invited Jesus saw what was happening, he said to himself, If this man were a prophet, he would know what kind of woman is touching him. He would know that she is a sinner.
>
> Jesus replied, "Simon, I have something to say to you."
>
> "Teacher, speak," he said.
>
> "A certain lender had two debtors. One owed enough money to pay five hundred people for a day's work. The other owed enough money for fifty. When they couldn't pay, the lender forgave the debts of them both. Which of them will love him more?"

> Simon replied, "I suppose the one who had the largest debt canceled."
> Jesus said, "You have judged correctly."
> Jesus turned to the woman and said to Simon, "Do you see this woman? When I entered your home, you didn't give me water for my feet, but she wet my feet with tears and wiped them with her hair. You didn't greet me with a kiss, but she hasn't stopped kissing my feet since I came in. You didn't anoint my head with oil, but she has poured perfumed oil on my feet. This is why I tell you that her many sins have been forgiven; so she has shown great love. The one who is forgiven little loves little."
> Then Jesus said to her, "Your sins are forgiven."
> The other table guests began to say among themselves, "Who is this person that even forgives sins?"
> Jesus said to the woman, "Your faith has saved you. Go in peace."

This woman knew that God's action toward her was an astonishing gift. She knew she had been forgiven of much, and that awareness fueled her outlandish expression of worship. She began with tears, which allowed her to wash Jesus' feet. Then she dried his feet with her hair. Then she kissed Jesus' feet before she anointed them with ointment. Her immense expression of love came from her profound sense of forgiveness. God acted through the person of Jesus; the woman responded with tears of gratitude. That's worship!

GOD'S ACTION: FUEL FOR WORSHIP

Now, let's return to the analogy of a jazz band backing up a soloist as he or she improvises. In our analogy, God is the soloist, and we are the backup musicians playing off of God's solo. In the two biblical stories we've just looked at, we can see that Jacob and the woman who washed Jesus' feet are doing exactly that. Neither of these stories takes place in a planned worship service. They are improvised moments that resulted from joining in with what God was doing.

If God's action is the fuel for worship, then the health and vibrancy of our worship will depend on how closely we are looking for God's grace in our lives. To be listening for God's improvised solo in our life, we must keep tuning our ear for that song. We must keep turning our attention toward God. We can call this a "Godward life."

The Godward life begins with the discovery that God is active in our world and wants to include us in that activity, with our specific gifts. We seek to discover how God's action is breaking into every corner of our lives and the world. We can name this the Godward life because we are repeatedly turning back toward God. This is the practice of the Godward life: turning back toward God moment by moment, day by day, throughout life.

We often forget to turn Godward in our living, but we can practice it just like we can practice anything else. If I want to run a marathon, I don't go out on the first day and run twenty-six miles. I start by running two miles, and I build up to twenty-six over many months. If I want to learn to play guitar, I don't start by playing an Eric Clapton solo. I start by learning individual chords. If I want to live the Godward life, I don't start by loving my enemies. I start by helping my friendly neighbors assemble their new grill. Eventually, we build up to loving our enemies—seriously.

Living a Godward life is simple but certainly not easy. It is difficult because God's guidance and action are not always obvious. There are seasons when we must wait for God's timing, and that can feel frustrating. There are also times when injustice, pain, suffering, and sin place a cloak over God's action.

When we are suffering, it is invaluable to know God is not inflicting suffering upon us. Instead, Jesus stands beside us in our suffering, for he understands exactly what it means to bear injustice, pain, suffering, and sin. He grieves with us. He understands our pain and doubt. And our hope is this: God is able to work through all these things to bring redemption and wholeness. But still, when the cloak of suffering is covering God's work, we struggle to believe God is active.

The Godward life can sound theological and abstract. But in fact, when we see someone else living it, we can't miss it. For me, one person who lived the Godward life was Judy.

When I first got to know Judy, she had just lost her home and was living in her car. She had several health issues, but her mind was brilliant and sharp. One evening, she shared with a few of us how she had been feeling so discouraged by her living situation. She was turning this over in her mind when she recalled a line from a song: "Count your blessings, name them one by one," so she began to think about each item she still possessed in her car.

As each item came to mind, Judy found herself becoming thankful for the item, the person who gave it to her, or what it provided to her. She was moved to gratitude and praise. And, thankfully, it wasn't too long before she was able to find a home.

A Powerful and Beautiful Picture

I specifically remember a friend of mine who was in the room when Judy told us about her many blessings. My friend was so thunderstruck by Judy's gratitude that she resolved to spend time every week with Judy and her circle of friends. Why was she so motivated? Because a person who is deeply rooted in the Godward life is inspiring to us.

If we have a clear picture of the Godward life in our minds, then it will be an exciting and energizing life to imagine. Being energized is helpful to us because it will motivate us to seek first the kingdom of God.

If our picture of the Godward life is one where we have to give up all of our favorite things and be miserable to make God like us, then we will run out of energy pretty quickly. We'll stop training to live this type of life. But if we are excited by the image of this life of deep intimacy and friendship with God, then we will have the motivation necessary to devote time and energy to what God is inviting us to discover.

In our hurried and scurried lives, many of us struggle to prioritize our lives with God. If you have ever committed to praying more, reading Scripture more, or having more worship time, and then promptly proceeded not to do that very thing, please don't beat yourself up about it. Instead, seek out a more powerful and compelling vision. Feeling guilty can be a helpful indicator that we are headed in the wrong direction, but it is a poor motivator.

The Best Life Possible

The fact is that living a Godward life that flows into worship is the most amazing life we could ever possibly live. Living a life where we can have the Creator, the Redeemer, and the Sustainer moving through each moment of each day with us is the greatest gift we could receive. Knowing that when we face any challenge we can turn and have a conversation with God about our struggles is astonishing.

Turning toward God means we can bring God's love and peace and healing into every relationship we have. It starts with the people we already care about, bringing greater and greater love into our relationships with them.

As Mother Teresa would say, we can do small gestures with great love. Yet, the Godward life doesn't stop there. It expands to impact our relationships with the people in our lives who are difficult to love because of what they have suffered or mistakes they have made. God's guidance and love make it possible for us to love them.

The Godward life also leads us into exciting and joyful discoveries about ourselves and our world. Learning how to follow God's leading could impact your work—how you work or where you work.

The Godward life could impact where we live. You might feel led to relocate to a place that the world has chosen to ignore. Or you might stay right where you are and intentionally foster love for your neighbors and love for where you live. The Godward life might guide you to creating art, poetry, music, or film. The Godward life might stir your heart to start a nonprofit around something you care deeply about, or it might guide you to enter into a specific ministry. The joyous possibilities are endless!

Worship and the Godward Life

Keep in mind, the fruit of this Godward life is worship. As we seek God's guidance and action in our lives and the world, we will discover it. And when we see what God is up to, we will naturally want to praise God.

Sometimes we will respond with awe, as Jacob did after his dream. Sometimes we will respond with tears of joy, as did the woman who washed Jesus' feet. Sometimes we will respond with gratitude, as Judy did after recounting what God had given her. Our worship can cover the full range of human emotion and experience because God is active in the full range of human emotion and experience.

CONCLUSION

I grew up with a fairly weak and watery understanding of jazz. Then, in my thirties, I was able to experience (emphasis: experience) jazz in New Orleans. It completely changed my understanding of the music and the culture surrounding jazz.

How many of us are living with a weak and watery understanding of worship? I suspect many of us are! But it doesn't have to stay this way. The Spirit beckons us to drop our shallow or false understandings of worship and step into the Godward life that can only result in worship.

Individually and with others, we can pursue this Godward and worshipful life. Small steps and simple practices can help us immensely.

Active Application

This chapter is packed with several big ideas that are foundational to our understanding of worship and the Godward life. However, we don't discover worship just by reading about it. We also discover a worshipful life by living it. We discover this life by practicing and experimenting. Below are a few practices to help you live into the Godward life more fully. They are suggestions, not assignments. The Godward life is a dynamic relationship with God, not a checklist of tasks. Prayerfully look over this list for the practice that catches your attention or stirs your curiosity. Use it as a starting place to discover your ability to fully experience worship.

Entering the Story

The primary Gospel passage of this chapter was Luke 7:36-50, the story of the woman washing Jesus' feet. To explore your own feelings about the Godward life and worship, you can prayerfully read this story and allow yourself to be part of it.

To begin, invite the Holy Spirit to open your heart so that God might speak to you through this passage. After the prayer, read the passage twice to get acquainted with the story. Then read the passage a third time, as any character in the story. You might be Simon the Pharisee, you might be the woman, you might be an unnamed observer.

Read the passage slowly and with pauses. During the pauses, picture the story in your mind. As you witness this act of adoration and worship, allow whatever feelings (pleasant or unpleasant) to rise to the surface. Invite Jesus to look into your heart and talk with you about what he finds there.

When you have finished this prayer time, take a few minutes to write down your reflections on the experience. Know that even if the prayer experience seems fruitless, God will be able to work through it. By reflecting on the experience, you have the opportunity to gain insight into God's work in your life.

Turning Godward (Prayer of Examen)

One of the simplest and most valuable ways we can cultivate the Godward life is by spending time each day noticing where God seemed present and where God appeared to be absent. This exercise is traditionally known as a prayer of examen.[4]

We trust that God desires to lead us through the small moments in our lives, as well as the "burning bush" moments. The prayer of examen gives us a chance to "dust for fingerprints" and see where God is working in our lives. We know that God has been at work in our lives when we experience fullness of life, healing, gratitude, and/or joy. Here is one way to practice this exercise:

The prayer of examen is generally done once a day (either at the end of the day or at the beginning).

Begin by lighting a candle and having a moment of silence, allowing yourself to remember that God is active and present in your life. Then, reflecting on the previous twenty-four hours (if you are doing this exercise daily), ask the Holy Spirit to guide you in answering these two questions:

- For what moment am I most thankful?
- For what moment am I least thankful?

As you answer each question, do not filter your thoughts. Allow yourself to be honest and open with God. As we do this practice, we are reminding ourselves that even the smallest moments of joy or gratitude are gracious gifts from a God who loves us. The moments we are thankful for are invitations, helping us know what direction God is leading us. And in the same way, the moments we are least thankful for can sometimes help us discover areas of our lives where we need to make changes.

Keep a journal of your answers. You need not write much in the journal; just a word or phrase will do. Over time, look back over your journal for any patterns forming that help you in knowing how best to cooperate with God.

Describe Your Godward Life

God is inviting you into an abundant and eternal type of life. One of the greatest ways to motivate ourselves for this Godward life is to describe what it might look like. (I say "might" because we can't know exactly what our life in Christ will look like, but that doesn't mean we can't move in that direction and learn as we go.)

For this exercise, write or draw an illustration that depicts what your life would look like if you lived moment by moment in dialogue with God. To begin, find a journal or a blank sheet of paper. Spend a few moments in prayer, asking the Holy Spirit to guide your imagining.

Then begin writing or drawing what your Godward life might look like. You might describe one specific day, you might describe what is happening inside you as you move through a normal day, or you might describe the type of character you develop as a result of following Jesus closely.

The goal of this exercise is to be inspired and energized to take action.

Questions for Personal Reflection and Group Discussion

1. The opening story helps create an analogy between a jazz band and a worshipful life. How does this analogy challenge and/or inspire your understanding of a worshipful life?

2. What do you find helpful about the author's definition of worship? What would you add to or take away from that definition (if anything)?

3. When you think of Jacob awaking from his dream and the woman washing Jesus' feet with her tears, what words would you use to describe their worship? Reflect on a time you engaged in worship in a way that was similar to either Jacob or the woman.

4. Which half-truth or fully false belief about worship do you most struggle to undo? Is there a half-truth you would add to the author's list?

5. When have you experienced worship outside a church building? How did that experience impact you?

6. Can you think of someone you have known personally who lived a Godward life? What was it about that person that made you think so?

CHAPTER 2

How Worship Forms Us

It was a warm and windy Labor Day weekend Sunday when I went to visit Resurrection Community Church. The church worships in my neighborhood; specifically, directly across the street from my office. Because of their proximity to my office, I had gotten to know their pastor, Riccardo Harris. He is a gifted leader and caring person. As with any church in my neighborhood, I'm always happy to find ways to partner together and let the neighborhood know what gifts that church brings to the community. In honor of that partnership, I wanted to join them for worship.

I admit, I was nervous as I walked into the church building. By the grace of God, Pastor Riccardo was walking toward the door just as I was walking in. He greeted me with a handshake and a hug and said, "It is good to see a familiar face." I felt my shoulders relax.

As I found a seat, the associate pastor, Pastor Woody, was beginning the service. He was sharing the Scripture God had placed on his heart, Philippians 3:12-14.

> It's not that I have already reached this goal or have already been perfected, but I pursue it, so that I may grab hold of it because Christ grabbed hold of me for just this purpose. Brothers and sisters, I myself don't think I've

> reached it, but I do this one thing: I forget about the things behind me and reach out for the things ahead of me. The goal I pursue is the prize of God's upward call in Christ Jesus.

Pastor Woody launched right into this Scripture by sharing his story. He shared openly about his struggles. He also explained that instead of looking back on his struggles, he was going to live into his new identity by pressing on toward Christ. He called us to live into our calling as beloved children of God, no longer our former selves, but instead our new selves which are created for praise. I immediately knew the Spirit had brought me to this worship service to teach me the importance of story in worship.

After Pastor Woody shared, the choir began to lead the singing. Each song was call-and-response. The lyrics were prayers expressing our longing for and discovering of God. Between the songs, individuals from the choir would tell stories from their week and what God was doing in their lives. The sharing was honest and powerful, and it changed the way I listened to the songs.

When the music ended, Pastor Riccardo's wife came forward and told a story of a specific way God had spoken into her life through prayer. Then, Pastor Riccardo stood up to give the message, but it wasn't a sermon as much as it was a story of his own experiences of feeling God was silent. He openly wondered how we remain faithful even in those seasons.

Moved by the Holy Spirit, Pastor Riccardo invited three people to come forward and share their own stories of how God had been meeting them throughout their days.

After the three who had arranged to share their stories were finished, Pastor Riccardo opened the floor for others to share what was on their hearts. As each person shared, people in the congregation would call out words of encouragement. And slowly, person by person, the stories of God working in individual lives were intertwined with each other's and, most importantly, with God's! When the service was over, nine different people had shared their stories. Their stories reminded all of us that God is at work in our lives; we just have to have eyes to see and ears to hear. When we realize God is at work in our lives, we have a reason to worship. And as we join with others to celebrate what God is doing, we are transformed.

HOW WE ARE FORMED

As human beings, we are constantly being formed. Our character is being shaped. Our souls are being molded by several factors. This is important because many people *feel* stuck with the character they have. But, in fact, they are not stuck with their character—it can be changed.

The marks of character include our integrity, our honesty, our values, and our inner dispositions. So, when I speak of changing our character, I'm not talking about becoming smarter, more attractive, wealthier, or more powerful. Instead, I am saying you can become the kind of person who operates from a place of love, joy, peace, generosity, and self-control.

There are three things that shape our character: our relationships, our stories, and our activities.[5]

Relationships

We are shaped by our relationships. And as those circles of relationships broaden, we are also shaped by our community. For some people, this is rather obvious; they are easily led by others and take on the beliefs of the strongest person in the room. But even for the strongest person in the room, there are community values and beliefs they have absorbed. We read the books that our friends suggest, we watch the television shows that our spouse enjoys, we work with the investment banker our coworker recommends, and so forth. All of these relationships have an influence on us and our character. If my family of origin believes the true measure of a person is how successful they are in their endeavors, then my character will be shaped around that idea.

Stories

And then there are the stories that shape us. We make sense of the world through our stories. We have our personal stories, the ones that hold deep meaning for us or pop into our heads when we least expect it. These could be just short memories that we carry from our past. There are also stories that are part of our community. When a church gets a new pastor, an important story may emerge. When a town experiences a natural disaster, a story is created. A foundational story for many is the Bible and all the smaller stories that make it up. These stories shape our understanding of who God is and what God is like.

There are also smaller stories that bombard us throughout the day in the form of advertisements and media. Some researchers estimate that we are exposed to five thousand ads a day . . . A DAY![6] In addition to being annoying, we need to ask: What is their story? The story of advertising is often our insufficiency and the promise of happiness through purchasing. How might that message be shaping us?

Activities

And finally, there are the activities we do. I've chosen the word *activities* because it is intentionally broad. Activities are the ways we spend our time. Our activities include our work, our hobbies, our practices—every choice and action we make throughout each day. They have a deep influence on our character. If we see our work as meaningful, it will help keep our character rooted. If we devote time to gardening, it will probably be good for our souls. If we give ourselves permission to learn new things, like a musical instrument or a craft, it will stimulate our minds. These are all gifts to us.

Relationship + Story + Activity = Character

It is an oversimplification, but we can say that putting relationship, story, and activity together shapes our character. Here is a concrete example. When I was twenty years old, I became friends with a guy at work named Scott who was about my age. He was a thrill-seeker who enjoyed skydiving and rock-climbing and rule-breaking. He convinced me to go skydiving, and even though I am not the kind of person who chases after the next adrenaline rush, I had a great time. Nowadays, when an opportunity comes up to do something a little bit exciting, the story of skydiving with Scott goes through my mind and I say, "Yes!" As a result, a friend recently described me as being unafraid in any situation. My relationship with Scott, our activity of going skydiving, and the story I have in my experience shape my character.

SPIRITUAL PRACTICES: ACTIVITIES FOR THE SOUL

As Christians, our relationships with God and with other Christians shape our character. The stories of the Bible and of others walking the Christian walk shape our character. And the activities we do that help us engage with our faith shape our character as well. We call these activities *spiritual practices*. Spiritual practices are activities that place us before God so that God might transform us. Some of the spiritual practices help us disengage from old mind-sets that are harmful to our character, such as greed, anger, lying, or lust. There are also spiritual practices which help us lean into new, Christ-centered mind-sets. The resulting characteristics might include living generously, encouraging others, speaking the truth in love, and honoring the inherent value in others.

Throughout the history of Christianity, there have been certain practices that have been acknowledged as especially helpful for people who are seeking to follow Jesus in their daily lives. That list would include (but is not limited to):

- Fasting
- Silence
- Solitude
- Simplicity
- Confession
- Prayer
- Study
- Service
- Discernment

And, of course, worship!

$$(\text{RELATIONSHIP}+\text{STORY}+\text{ACTIVITY})^{\text{HOLY SPIRIT}} = \text{TRANSFORMATION}$$

When we bring these three things together and place them in God's hands, truly beautiful things happen. Understanding that the spiritual practices are all about our relationship with God and how God is speaking a new story into our lives takes the gray scale television of religion and turns it into a vibrant, real-life experience!

It is helpful to think of this in comparison to other meaningful relationships. For example, my wife, Catherine, and I are together most of the time when we aren't at work. But during our twenty years of marriage, we have learned that it is helpful to have regular times dedicated and protected for us to just be together. So, we have seasons when we have a monthly date night. We also observe a weekly sabbath (most weeks, but not always) and during that time, we rest, read aloud, share coffee, or catch up on life. These intentional times of connection help deepen the connection we share as we move through the hustle and bustle of life.

In the same way, we can do spiritual practices like Bible study, Scripture meditation, fasting, prayer, and yes, worship to deliberately be with God. This is for our benefit. We know that God is always with us—whether we are worshipping or washing the dishes. But for some of us, it is easy to forget God is present when we wash the dishes. But if we have a time of worship in the morning, then when we wash the dishes after breakfast, we might be more aware of God's loving presence.

Interacting with God is going to change us. That relationship is going to set us free, and it is going to make us whole. We know that God is not passive about our formation. Because God loves us so much, God has a deep and profound desire for us to be whole and joyous. God's desire for us is revealed beautifully when Jesus (God Incarnate) reads in the synagogue what could be described as his mission statement:

> The Spirit of the Lord is upon me,
> because the Lord has anointed me.
> He has sent me to preach good news to the poor,
> to proclaim release to the prisoners
> and recovery of sight to the blind,
> to liberate the oppressed,
> and to proclaim the year of the Lord's favor.
> (Luke 4:18-19)

When we spend time with God, God desires to speak good news into our lives, to release us from that which has trapped us, to help us see in new ways, to lift off that which is oppressing us, and to show us the Lord's favor.

Being in relationship with God not only leads to greater freedom, it also leads to greater wholeness as we begin to absorb and reveal the character of God. Again, we see this truth revealed in our other relationships: we are shaped by the people we spend time with. Again, I return to my relationship with Catherine, and I would point out that during our marriage, I have become more like her in the way I view finances (well-managed). And she has become more like me in the way she makes the bed (only when completely necessary).

Certainly, if we are spending intentional time with God, we begin to reflect the characteristics of God. And this is good news because God is loving, patient, merciful, generous, and wise. We can grow into people who are generous of heart, forgiving, just, and compassionate. This is the abundant life that Jesus has made available to us. It is robust, bold, and meaningful. It is the life we were created to live.

THE IMPORTANCE OF INTENTION

Practicing the spiritual practices doesn't automatically result in the life we may desire or the life God desires us to live. Indeed, some have been practicing the spiritual practices their whole lives, but aren't living an abundant life. A quick glance at the Gospels will reveal that people can be very disciplined and yet also not be very loving. The Pharisees are an astonishingly disciplined group, and yet they cannot grasp Jesus' actions which are guided by love. And sadly, we need look no further than our own congregations to find modern-day Pharisees. There are individuals who attend worship and Sunday school every week, ongoing Bible studies, and committees . . . and yet, they are flat-out mean to people. I recently heard of a man who was a lifelong member of his church and participated in multiple ways. And yet, he was so cutting in his comments toward other people, no one was willing to work with him at an annual church event. Ironically, one of his great complaints was that no one would ever help him with anything.

Let's be clear, though: our job is not to judge people. It is impossible for us to know the heart of another and what transformation and healing may be happening within, while externally we can't see this change happening. But it is important to be aware that we can do the spiritual practices in such a way that we are not transformed. In fact, we can do the spiritual practices in such a way that it is harmful for our souls, and we become less Christlike. In order to stay clear of this mistake, we must be very clear of our goal. Practicing the spiritual practices is not the goal. Going through the action is not why we do the spiritual practices. Going to worship is not the goal. We go to worship *so that we can be transformed.* The goal of the spiritual practices is to open ourselves up to God, to deepen our relationship with Jesus, to live Godward, and to become Spirit-led people who are growing in love of God and neighbor. This is our goal, and we must be intentional in pursuing that goal.

When we are unintentional with the spiritual practices, they can become destructive. We can misuse them to prove that we are better than other people. We can misuse them to isolate ourselves. We can misuse them in an effort to earn God's love. We can misuse them to build up our little ego. We can even misuse them to deafen ourselves to God's voice.

Intentionality is the act of remembering why we are showing up. To be intentional is to be deliberate and purposeful with our actions. It is natural for us as humans to seek routine and remove intentionality. But when we remove intentionality from our spiritual life, those lives become a checklist of routines rather than acts of love in a meaningful relationship. And so, we want to keep reminding ourselves that the goal of all of our spiritual practices is to deepen our relationship with God.

STAY ALERT

Jesus does not use the word *intention* in the Gospels, but he does talk about being alert. In Luke 12:35-38, Jesus speaks about servants who are prepared for their master's return.

> Be dressed for service and keep your lamps lit. Be like people waiting for their master to

> come home from a wedding celebration, who can immediately open the door for him when he arrives and knocks on the door. Happy are those servants whom the master finds waiting up when he arrives. I assure you that, when he arrives, he will dress himself to serve, seat them at the table as honored guests, and wait on them. Happy are those whom he finds alert, even if he comes at midnight or just before dawn.

Jesus is inviting us to be awake, to be ready. And while we often assume this passage is about the end of the world, I believe it is applicable to every moment of our lives. Are we awake and ready for God's presence to show up? Are we alert when we show up to worship or are we sleepwalking through our lives, unaware that Jesus is knocking at the door regularly? Are we living a Spirit-led, Godward life?

> Active Application
>
> *Many worship services are packed with language to help us set our intention and remember why we are showing up. With elements such as a "call to worship," a "greeting," and an "opening hymn," we are given a chance to see why we have gathered together as the people of God. The next time you attend a worship service of any type, look for elements of worship that help you set your intention on God. How does noticing these elements impact your preparation for and experience of worship?*

How Worship Forms Us

When I went to worship at Resurrection Community Church, I witnessed how God is able to work through worship to shape our lives. The joy, hope, and goodness of that worshipping community is a testimony that God is at work in that place. It also reveals that worship offers us specific ways to be formed into Christlikeness, and it is a wonderful list. Of course, other spiritual practices also offer these ways of being formed, but it is worth noting special gifts that worship can bring into our lives.

God-centered Experience

The first gift that worship offers to us is the chance to not be the center of the universe. Instead, it is the joyous chance to let God be the center of the universe for a bit. It is so exhausting to live life as if we are the center of everything. In our souls, we sense that the whole story can't just be about us: what we like, dislike, want, don't want, and so forth. In worship, we have the opportunity for a short time to focus on asking: What does God like? What does God want? How is God the center of this story?

This is a major shift in perspective, and I am convinced it leads to abiding joy. While it is appropriate for God to be the center of the universe and every story, God is also love and longs to include us in the story. God longs to include our gifts, our struggles, our hopes, our desires in the story. So, to place God at the center is not to exclude ourselves completely, but instead, we operate from a place of relationship with God.

Active Application: Arrive early for worship and let go of your own agenda.

Make a practice to arrive early to your place of worship. Spend a few minutes in quiet, praying for the worship leaders and all those who will be participating in worship. Then spend a few minutes calling to mind that God is the center of worship. This might mean releasing your own agenda for worship. Or it could mean turning your attention more fully toward God. Seek to turn your heart toward God in such a way that your desire is seeking God's desire.

REMEMBERING GOD'S STORY

As I mentioned earlier, we are story beings. We make sense of the world with stories. And in this regard, worship is vitally important because it is an opportunity to hear the story of God's work throughout human history as well as our own individual lives and the lives of those who are connected to us.

It is formative to hear the story of God's work because if we don't hear that story, we will either make up our own story or absorb the cultural story of what God is doing. And we live according to our stories. This means we make decisions and take actions based on the stories we believe. If I absorb the cultural story of a god who has given up on the world and is waiting at a distance until we have screwed things up so badly that we can only be punished, then I am going to make decisions accordingly. I will live with fear and anxiety, believing God is distant and I am completely on my own with no help or hope.

In contrast, if I hear the gospel story of a God who shows up in unexpected places and is fully present to pain and brings healing and wholeness, then I begin to grow in my faith and make decisions that are hopeful. I begin looking for God's actions popping up in places I never thought they would pop up. I must hear the stories again and again in order to really start to believe them.

So, let's tell God's story because it is a beautiful and life-giving story to tell and to live by! Whether we gather in a large congregation with thousands of worshippers or we gather with two or three others in our living room for praise and prayer, we can still tell the story. And we can listen well. When we realize the importance these stories have on our lives, we give greater intentionality to our listening.

I am convinced this is the reason Jesus told his disciples to eat bread and drink wine in remembrance of him. The act of taking Communion gives us a chance to gather around the Table and remember the story of God-in-flesh, who came into our world, taught, healed, wept, and suffered. He was rejected by those in power who put him to death, and on the cross, it looked like all hope was gone—love had lost. But then on the third day, he was raised. The tomb was empty, and Jesus' followers were shocked to discover that love is even stronger than death. The more that we can absorb that story, the more we grow in being able to let love win, even when it seems hopeless. Why? Because we know the story.

Second, when we continually tell God's story, we not only remember the greater arc of God's story, but we also remember what God has done in our own lives. This is important in seasons of waiting when we can't see what God is doing. I recently lived this out in a microscopic way that convinced me how true it is.

One winter day, I found myself struggling to do anything. I was ready to stay in my rocking chair all day. I was weighed down with the sadness and struggle of life, overwhelmed by the work I saw laid out in front of me of connecting neighbors and building community. But in a moment of grace, it occurred to me that I could recount the ways I had seen God at work in my neighborhood. I literally started telling myself those stories, and slowly I discovered that my hopefulness was restored. I was encouraged in my despair by remembering the story of God's work that I had experienced in my own life. Now, this is not meant to imply that we can solve all of our problems just by telling these stories to ourselves. And for those who struggle with depression, know that I'm not implying doing this exercise will take all your trouble away. I was not struggling with depression, just feeling down. But remembering pulled me out.

Third, we grow as people who seek first the kingdom of God (Matthew 6:33). Jesus speaks of the kingdom of God in present tense (Mark 1:14) and describes it as those moments when God's will is being done (hence, the line in the Lord's Prayer, "Thy kingdom come, thy will be done"). So, when we tell stories of what God has done throughout history and in our own lives, we are telling stories about the kingdom of God. These stories, in turn, help us to know what we are looking for as we move out into the world.

As an example, we can hear again and again the parable that the kingdom of God is like yeast mixed into a measure of dough (Matthew 13:33). If we start to absorb that story into our lives, an interesting thing begins to happen. We start to become more vigilant for those small, almost hidden acts of love and generosity. We become more sensitive to individuals who seem to operate with no ego agenda, but instead, simply do what they feel is right. We do this because those folks are like leaven that has been mixed into the dough. They keep going about their business, but the fact remains that they are having an impact on the people around them. To seek first the kingdom of God is to live the Godward life.

Active Application: Remembering God's Story

Before worship begins, spend a few minutes reflecting on the previous week. Ask yourself, if you could tell a story in worship of what God did in your life this week, what would you share? It doesn't have to be dramatic or impressive. In fact, there may be areas of doubt and uncertainty; that is part of the journey.

Nevertheless, practicing telling your story (even if it is only in your own head) is a powerful way to remember God's story. And if you have it prepared in your mind, you may be more inclined to share that story with others in your life.

NEW IDENTITY

Worship also offers a wonderful combination of story and relationship as we live into our new identity as beloved children of God. When we worship, we tell the story of God adopting us and we experience our relationship with God as the result of that adoption. Romans 8 reminds us that we have not received a spirit of fear, but instead we have received a spirit of adoption. We have been brought into a deeper relationship with God, and that deepening relationship is our story.

It is extremely important that we know our identity as beloved children of God. But it is also difficult to grasp our new identity and how we live from that new identity.

Whether we know it or not, we often build our identity around the things we do well and the things we do poorly. For example, when I was in high school, I held on tightly to my identity as a musician because I was one of the best musicians in my school. (I overlooked the fact that there were only fifteen people in concert band.) I built an identity which could be summarized as "musician." That identity was based on something I did well, and it gave me a sense of security.

As odd as it might sound, we can also experience a sense of security from negative identities. After college, I got a job in youth ministry and that was a very difficult position for me. I struggled to connect with youth, and I struggled to expand the youth program.

As a result, I began to view my identity as one of a failure. This career struggle, along with other setbacks in life, left me feeling as if everything I touched failed. Hence, I felt like my identity was "loser."

This identity began to impact my life story and my relationship with God. It impacted my life story because whenever I thought about doing something, the story of my past failures would rise up and I would reach the conclusion that the future will be no different than the past. During this same season of life, I felt like God had grown silent, and my conclusion to that experience was that God had given up on me because everything I did failed.

Worship provides space for God to speak a different story into our lives. Worship is a chance to discover a very different reality: our identity is not based on our successes or our failures; it is based on God's love for us. God is the central character of our story. Our successes and failures do not define us; God's love does. This does not mean success is bad, and it doesn't mean we can't learn from our failures. It simply means that those do not determine who we are.

Worship on Christmas Eve especially reminds me of this new identity God gives us. One particular year, I was helping lead worship. I was sitting in the front of the church while a group of teenagers carried candles into the darkened sanctuary. As the light entered the darkened room, I was reminded of the God who loves us so much that God became a tiny, defenseless baby entering into the darkness of struggle, pain, and violence that is all around us. As each candle was carried into the sanctuary, my eyes welled up with tears of gratitude. I found myself joining the angels, the shepherds, the wise men, the cattle and sheep, and Joseph and Mary in welcoming the newborn King. Not only does this reveal what God is like, but it also reveals how much God loves us.

What happens as we learn to live into this new identity? We live differently. We live a Godward life that impacts the world around us. And this is another way that worship forms us.

Active Application: Breath Prayer

Breath prayer is an ancient Christian practice that allows us to pray without ceasing. It is also a powerful way to recognize our new identity in Christ. A breath prayer is built with two short phrases. The first phrase is said, or thought, on the inhale, and the second phrase is said, or thought, on the exhale.

An example, which is also the oldest Christian breath prayer would be this:

Inhale: Lord, Jesus Christ,
Exhale: have mercy on me.

But you can build your own by allowing the inhale to be your dearest name for God, such as Abba, Jesus, Spirit, Love, Elohim, Lord, Rabbi, *and so forth. The exhale is then your deepest longing for God. This phrase could be something like "have mercy" or "help me" or "thank you."*

Because we have been exploring our new identity in Christ, I would encourage you to use a breath prayer that invites that new identity to take root in your mind and life. Here are some examples:

Inhale: Lord, Jesus Christ,
Exhale: I am yours.
Inhale: Holy Spirit,
Exhale: set me free.
Inhale: Abba Father,
Exhale: I am your child.

You can say your breath prayer anytime, anywhere. People have shared with me that they use their breath prayer at red lights while they are waiting. Other people have used their breath prayer each time they take a break from their work. To say a breath prayer for a minute several times during the day can help us remember that we have been adopted into the family of God.

NEW BEHAVIOR IN THE WORLD

One morning I was teaching a class at the nearby university, Friends University. I was teaching a course on spiritual formation and the role of the spiritual practices in shaping our lives. It was a lively group, even though it was early in the morning. And it was early in the semester as well. I was working through several discussion points, which is normal at the beginning of the semester as I seek to set a foundation for the weeks ahead. There was a lot of ground to cover. We had concluded one topic, and I was quickly transitioning to the next, when a woman in the back of the room raised her hand and apologized for interrupting me.

She was a nontraditional student. In a class full of eighteen- and nineteen-year-olds, she had just turned seventy. She had decided to pursue one of her lifelong dreams of becoming a writer, so she enrolled in classes, which were free because of her age. She was a joyful, encouraging woman, with wisdom to share and a personality that made you want to receive it.

After apologizing for interrupting me, she said, "Professor Johnson, I would like to read one quote from our reading because I thought it was just so important." I encouraged her to do so, and then she read these words from Leo Tolstoy, "Everybody thinks of changing humanity and nobody thinks of changing himself." The class grew quiet as we absorbed those words, which I had so conveniently glossed over time and again. The student smiled and said, "That is so true and so beautiful; I just wanted us to hear it out loud." Indeed!

That moment has stayed with me as I have come to realize how desperately humanity desires change and how tempting it is to expect everyone else to change rather than me. But if I pursue transformation, I can become the change I long to see in the world. And perhaps some of it wears off on the people around me as well. I certainly know that the characteristics of others rub off on me!

And so it is with worship. Remember our definition for worship: it is the spiritual practice of responding to God's action. We have intentional time with God, so that the character of God might rub off on us. As Paul wrote in Ephesians 5, "Therefore, imitate God like dearly loved children. Live your life with love, following the example of Christ, who loved us and gave himself for us. He was a sacrificial offering that smelled sweet to God" (verses 1-2).

As beloved children, we are invited to imitate God, which is a very good thing to do. And this naturally fits into the flow that exists around worship:

- We equip ourselves for worship by watching for what God is doing in our lives and the world.
- We enter worship and hear again and again the stories of how God moves into the neighborhood.
- As we participate in worship, we are putting on the character of Christ, the new self which is being given to us through the spirit of adoption, helping us be rooted and grounded in love.
- We go into the world with our eyes opened, seeking to participate in what God is doing.

We enter the world hopeful, joyful, reconciling, just, and generous. We don't enter the world with these characteristics because we are trying really hard to be hopeful. We enter the world this way because our minds, our perspectives have been transformed. Paul describes it with these words in Ephesians 4:23-24: "Renew the thinking in your mind by the Spirit and clothe yourself with the new person created according to God's image in justice and true holiness."

Rather than hating the world, we are moved by love for the world. We become the change we long to see in the world as we grow in loving people more deeply. The world is changed as we are transformed by God's love and begin to share that love with others and all creation. I genuinely believe this is what the world needs most: changed people.

As we engage in the story-changing, relationship-building practice of worship, we begin to develop characteristics that are shaped by God's character, characteristics like that of hope, joy, reconciliation, justice, and generosity.

Hopeful

The first characteristic to explore is hopefulness. It would be inaccurate to describe God as hopeful, because to hope is to believe in a good outcome which we cannot yet see. God is eternal and therefore doesn't have to hope for a good outcome, but instead is already present there as well. But as children of God who are hearing the story of how God works through "all things together for good for the ones who love God" (Romans 8:28), we do have hope that the future will be what God wills; in other words, it will be good. God is faithful and life-giving, therefore we are hopeful. And honestly, this can look pretty crazy.

I recently was praying through Psalm 56 and considering how hopeful its words are. I was pondering who I know that feels hopeless to me, and I pictured a friend of mine who struggles with addiction. As I considered her journey and her struggle, I recognized how hopeless I felt about it. And yet, I also know that even in a situation of repeated relapse, deception, and brokenness, God is able to do infinitely more than I can ask or imagine. I may or may not witness this transformation, but I know it is possible.

Joyful

God is joyful, and as God's children we grow in our joyfulness. As we become more rooted and grounded in love, we are able to see things with a wider perspective. We take ourselves a little less seriously. And we are able to take setbacks in stride. I have found it helpful to delineate between joy and happiness. Happiness is a passing emotion based on pleasure. It isn't bad, but it is temporary. Joy, on the other hand, is rooted in eternity and therefore is not shaken. I have often found that people who have suffered more than me also reveal a joy much greater than mine.

A Godward life is the most real life we can live. It is substantial in the way it satisfies our soul, leaving us content and joyful. This is in contrast to so much busyness and activity that leaves us dissatisfied and disappointed, longing for more. As I've talked with people who are growing in the Godward life, I have discovered that their old ways of distracting and numbing themselves are no longer interesting to them. Sometimes this means they are less drawn to things that can be destructive or unhealthy, like drugs or alcohol. And sometimes it just means they are less interested in the normal stuff of the modern world.

They watch less television, fewer sporting events, and movies; play less video games, indulge in less unhealthy eating. But notably, they are not throwing these things out because they are "bad." They just aren't as interesting as the very real adventure that is their life with God.

Reconciling

What the Gospels reveal to us in a most astonishing way is that God desires to overcome any gap to be in relationship with us. Jesus goes again and again to spend time with people who are considered "unclean" and "sinners." He joins them at their dining room tables, he touches them, he lets them touch him! And through these interactions, Jesus changes people's lives. Likewise, as we come to know ourselves as reconciled children of God, we grow in our ability to see how God desires to be reconciled with others. As we read in 2 Corinthians 5:18-20:

> All of these new things are from God, who reconciled us to himself through Christ and who gave us the ministry of reconciliation. In other words, God was reconciling the world to himself through Christ, by not counting people's sins against them. He has trusted us with this message of reconciliation. So we are ambassadors who represent Christ. God is negotiating with you through us. We beg you as Christ's representatives, "Be reconciled to God!"

Reconciliation is defined as "the process of making two people or groups of people friendly again after they have argued seriously or fought and kept apart from each other."[7] Humanity lives with a deeply rooted false narrative that God is against us, and therefore does not long to be with us. We have been given the beautiful opportunity to tell the true story, the story of a God who loves us enough to come to us. As this story is proclaimed, reconciliation is a natural result.

Just

Worship includes a life orientation of facing in a Godward direction, always listening and watching for God so that we can join in and respond. This helps us find the justice element of worship, because if we are turning Godward, then we will begin to see God at work in the world, and God desires justice.

When we speak of justice, we can understand it in a multitude of ways. It can include the element of fairness in our relationships and interactions. It can also include the common good for our neighbor, our neighborhood, our community, and beyond. One of the great struggles of our age is that as we become increasingly aware of the web of relationships that connects us with the rest of the world, we also carry the burden of injustice of which we were previously unaware. Our growth rate of awareness often feels faster than the rate at which we can change our behavior.

So, for example, when I become aware that the T-shirts I buy are made by underpaid children in a developing country, I can stop buying those shirts and begin buying them from a company that pays its workers a fair wage. But when these elements of injustice extend on into the food I eat, the car I drive, the products my company produces, where I live, how I entertain myself, and/or how my government acts on the global stage, that can be overwhelming.

Nevertheless, God is a just God. And more importantly, worship helps us to remember that we are called to pursue justice, and even as we struggle to do so, we are beloved children of God. We return to our identity and, from there, seek appropriate behavior which is reflective of God.

Generous

Finally, we grow as people with generous hearts because we love and serve a God who is generous. When we live life without God's love at the center of our lives, we struggle to be generous. How can I possibly be generous when there is no one watching out for me but me? At best, I might share with others once I have a surplus, but it will only be the extra that I share. All this changes when we discover that so much of life is a wondrous gift! The air we breathe, the water we drink, the friendships we have, the warmth and energy of the sun, the beauty of creation, the fact that we are even alive—these are all given to us! And we can savor and enjoy even the simplest gifts as expressions of a God who loves us.

Zacchaeus the tax collector was deeply transformed by his encounter with Jesus and was able to proclaim: "Look, Lord, I give half of my possessions to the poor. And if I have cheated anyone, I repay them four times as much" (Luke 19:8). When we have encounters with our loving and generous God, we are set free to live more generously.

Active Application: Cultivate one of the characteristics: hope, joy, reconciliation, justice, or generosity.
Prayerfully reflect on the characteristics of God we have named. Ask the Holy Spirit if there is one that could be increased in your life. If something comes to your attention, spend time in conversation with God about it. How might this aspect of your

character be developed? Is there a small practice you could do that would help it grow in your life? Perhaps there are passages of Scripture you could study around that topic. Perhaps there is a book about joy, hope, or abundance that you could read. Simply pay attention, and trust that the Spirit will bring you what you need.

TRANSFORMED TO REVEAL GOD'S KINGDOM

The folks at Resurrection Community Church helped me to see that worship is about telling the story of our relationship with God. It is the activity of turning toward God again and again. They also helped me see that worshipping God changes us. We are set free from our old prisons to run joyfully into the kingdom of God. They also helped me understand that while our changed behavior is a benefit to us, it is not for us alone. While we know Jesus came to give us his peace and abundant life, we also know he came to reveal the kingdom of God. As our behavior is transformed, we grow into the type of people who also reveal the kingdom of God. This is a blessing to those who interact with us. And just as Jesus taught, we become salt and light, so that others might see our good works and glorify our Father in heaven (Matthew 5:16).

Questions for Personal Reflection and Group Discussion

1. What relationships, stories, and activities currently shape your life? Which ones do you want to shape your being more?

2. What worship experiences stand out in your life? How have those worship experiences formed you?

3. Think for a moment about the bad news that you hear, the areas of your life where you feel trapped, the blind spots of your heart, the things that oppress you, and the ways in which you view God as being against you. If God were to begin changing those areas, bringing freedom and healing, what would your life be like? How might it be different?

4. If you had to explain the importance of intentionality to someone, what would you say?

5. Review the list of characteristics that we begin to develop as we grow in Christlikeness (hopeful, joyful, reconciling, just, and generous). Which of these have you found growing in your own life as you have grown closer to God? Which one do you long to see increased in your life? Why?

6. How might you become a minister of reconciliation? How might you speak truth? How might you address injustices of the world?

CHAPTER 3

Worship and Revealing God's Kingdom in the World

I recently had the opportunity to travel to the island of Iona in Scotland. The island is small, stretching four miles from north to south, and just one mile across. East of the island you can see Scotland, and the view to the west is the wide-open, tumultuous Atlantic Ocean. I traveled to Iona with a small group of people to experience the beauty and quiet of Iona, and also to visit the Christian community that lives and worships there.

The community came into being during the Great Depression. Presbyterian minister George MacLeod was serving in Glasgow, Scotland, and recognized that unemployment was killing the souls of the men around him, so he decided to come up with work for them to do that would utilize their skills as shipbuilders. His solution was to take a group of craftsmen and pastors-in-training out to the island of Iona to rebuild the abandoned abbey. There on the island, the group discovered the power of living with a daily rhythm of work and worship. Over the years, they began to write their own worship materials, such as prayers, liturgies,[8] and songs, which were based on what they felt God was calling them to do in the world.[9]

Today on the island of Iona, these worship materials are used twice a day in the fully-revived abbey, which the shipbuilders began renovating eighty years ago. The building is called the Iona Abbey. Worship happens there every morning and every night and includes Scripture, silence, prayer, singing, and very powerful liturgy. The beauty of the worship draws participants into a posture of praising God.

When I arrived in Iona, I did not know what to expect, and as it turned out, that was a very good thing. Normally, the island is host to almost 100 interns who are there to assist with worship and learn about the community. They are gifted musicians and worship leaders providing voice and instrumentation to the worship services. However, when I was there, the lodging facilities for the interns were being remodeled, which meant there were no interns living on the island. Instead of the morning and evening worship being filled with 125 people (100 of whom would be interns), they had 25 people. Most of the 25, like myself, did not know the songs or the liturgy. It was a mess, and it was a divine gift! It was a gift because it helped me see the purest, unadorned version of the Iona worship. Nothing fancy or impressive, but instead, humble, simple, and sparse like the Iona landscape.

There were so many phrases, prayers, and lyrics that spoke to me, but here is one that illustrates what I mean:

> **Leader: Where are you, God?**
>
> **All: You are present where women and men of good will still choose to live in your way, caring for creation and for each other, courageously speaking truth to power.**

You are there when elderly people share their wisdom.

You are there when street children dance in the rain.

You are present wherever, in this broken world, hope is alive.

Thank you, God, for being present with us now.

Amen.[10]

Even now when I read these words, I feel my heart rising with a deep desire to go out into the world. To seek God's will in my life and the world. To care for creation and the people around me. To speak truth to power in a way that is compassionate. To listen to the elderly and absorb their wisdom. To be present to the children of my community and witness their joy. To stand, alive with hope, in a broken world because God is present.

What I found so inspiring about the gathered worship on Iona was that it reminded me of what God is doing in our world and how we are created to collaborate with God in that work. That work involves bringing restoration, reconciliation, justice, and peace to a hurting world. I left the island of Iona with a greater appreciation of what can happen when people worship together regularly and are reminded of the calling God has placed on our lives. This was my "aha moment" for worship. It was because of my time in Iona that I agreed to write this book!

WORSHIP AND WORLD

There is a powerful and beautiful synergy that happens when we discover worship as a spiritual practice whereby we respond to what God is doing in our lives. We show up to worship to testify to what

God has done in our lives, but we aren't alone. Others join us. We hear songs of God's faithfulness, we hear Scriptures that reveal God's meta-story, and we hear the individual stories of our companions.

Then we enter the world and we have the opportunity to embody the characteristics of hope, joy, reconciliation, justice, and generosity. As we do so, we discover God meeting us in our everyday lives, giving us insight, wisdom, resources, and power as we face various moments throughout the day. Generally speaking, we do not discover God's activity in our lives immediately. It is revealed slowly and subtly. With time, we gradually cooperate with God more readily and grow in our awareness of God's presence.

We also then have the opportunity to join in the creative work that God is doing in our world. As Pierre Teilhard de Chardin writes, "To worship is now becoming to devote oneself body and soul to the creative act, associating oneself with that act in order to fulfill the world by hard work and intellectual exploration."[11]

If we live a daily life like this with God, then showing up for a worship gathering is a very different experience. We are energized to come together and share what we have been learning from God. And this brings us back to our first step, engaging in worship as the practice of responding to what God is doing in our lives. We are even more aware of how our own stories mirror the stories we hear from Scripture, from history, and from those joining us in worship.

Again and again, this pattern of seeking God, worshipping God, seeking God, worshipping God, seeking God, worshipping God reinforces our new identity in Christ and our calling. Jesus' way of capturing both our identity and our calling was to call us salt and light—to be salt and light in the world. That phrase, "salt and light," comes from Matthew 5:13, in the midst of the Sermon on the Mount. There, Jesus says,

> You are the salt of the earth. But if salt loses its saltiness, how will it become salty again? It's good for nothing except to be thrown away and trampled under people's feet.

Eugene Peterson gives a joyful interpretation of this passage in *The Message*. He interprets Matthew 5:13a this way: "Let me tell you why you are here. You're here to be salt-seasoning that brings out the God-flavors of this earth." If we keep in mind that God is patient and kind, not envious, boastful, arrogant, rude, irritable, or resentful, but instead rejoices in the truth and never ends, we can see why bringing out the "God-flavors of this earth" is such a good thing to be doing.[12]

Jesus moves on from describing us as salt to describing us as light in verses 14-16 (CEB):

> You are the light of the world. A city on top of a hill can't be hidden. Neither do people light a lamp and put it under a basket. Instead, they put it on top of a lampstand, and it shines on all who are in the house. In the same way, let your light shine before people, so they can see the good things you do and praise your Father who is in heaven.

I love that last phrase, "so *they* can see the good things you do and praise your Father who is in heaven." Those around us see our goodness, and they join in the worship of celebrating who God is. And we have the joy of being a finger pointing to God, inviting people to see what God is really like.

WHAT IS THE KINGDOM OF GOD?

The phrase, "the kingdom of God," was not a phrase I heard very much when I was growing up or first in ministry. I was more familiar with the phrase, "the kingdom of heaven," because I grew up hearing that Jesus was primarily focused on taking away our sins so we could go to heaven when we died. Therefore, it made sense that the "kingdom of heaven" was just a fancy way of talking about the afterlife. As it turns out, this is an insufficient understanding of the phrase, "the kingdom of heaven" as well as "the kingdom of God."

So, what *is* the kingdom of God?

First, the kingdom of God is the primary focus of Jesus' ministry. He speaks about the kingdom of God nearly one hundred times in total throughout the four Gospels. That is a lot of references. And yet, by the same token, Jesus is very vague about the kingdom of God. This is informative for us today. I have concluded that the very phrase, "the kingdom of God," is designed to elicit the question, "What is the kingdom of God?" When we ask that question, it helps us lean into the teachings of Jesus in a whole new way.

Second, because we can grow by asking what the kingdom of God is, I believe Jesus is very intentional in not giving a clear-cut definition of the kingdom of God. Instead, I see Jesus' teachings about the Kingdom as honoring the mystery of what the kingdom of God is. By mystery, I don't mean the kingdom of God is unknowable. Instead, I mean we can know a lot about the kingdom of God, but there will always be more to learn. It is an inexhaustible topic.

JESUS' OPENING PROCLAMATION

The first time Jesus uses the phrase, "kingdom of God," in the NRSV translation is in Mark 1:15. In his opening proclamation, he says, "The time is fulfilled, and the kingdom of God has come near; repent, and believe in the good news." It is fascinating to split this verse apart and look at it more closely. By doing so, we can see how meaningful these words are for us today. "The time is fulfilled" is a phrase of anticipation. By using this phrase, Jesus links his ministry and message to everything in human history that has led up to this. At a sporting event, the announcer will sometimes proclaim, "This is the moment you have all been waiting for!" When Jesus says, "The time is fulfilled," he is saying, "This is the time that all of humanity has been waiting for!" It is meant to stir the heart and heighten our awareness.

Then he tells us, "the kingdom of God has come near." For many years, I misread this phrase and thought Jesus was talking about time. In that way, his words were more of a threat, warning us to get ready. But Jesus is talking about distance. He is saying the reign of God is accessible to us. The kingdom of God is not high up and far away; it is coming near. This is further clarified with the other way the NRSV interprets this phrase. They note that it could also say, "The kingdom of God is at hand," implying that you can reach out and touch it. The kingdom of God is a present reality that is within our reach.

And then Jesus uses the word *repent*. Growing up, I thought that word meant "straighten up!" and that made sense in light of my other misunderstanding about the passage (that the kingdom of God was impending in the near future). But the Greek word for repent is *metanoia*. It literally means "change your mind." In other words, change the way you look at the world. Jesus is inviting us to look at the world as if God's kingdom were accessible to us, reachable and available. In other words, believe the good news!

To repent and believe the good news is not just a change in thinking; it is a change in the way we live our lives. In fact, the CEB translates this passage as just that: "Change your hearts and lives, and trust this good news!" This does not mean the purity police are coming around to check your behavior. No, the change of life means that we no longer live our lives as if we are alone in a cold, dark universe. And if you think about it, most sinful behavior is rooted in this illusion. If I believe I am alone in a cold, dark universe, then I am going to be greedy, fearful, selfish, and mean because the universe is terrifying.

But what if we aren't isolated and alone in a cold, dark universe? What if God is near to us and is seeking to stand beside us, even in the most difficult times? We can operate very differently. We don't have to operate as if we are the center of the universe striving to survive. Instead, we can be ruled by love. This becomes very specific. Instead of being greedy, we can be generous. Instead of being fearful, we can be open and loving. Instead of being selfish, we can be guided by love (which includes caring for ourselves and for others). Instead of being egocentric, we can be worshipful, celebrating who God is and what God has done. All this becomes possible as we grow in understanding that the kingdom of God is a way of life that is available to us right now.

If this type of life sounds amazing to you, then we can understand why Jesus would say, "The kingdom of heaven is like a treasure that somebody hid in a field, which someone else found and covered up. Full of joy, the finder sold everything and bought that field" (Matthew 13:44). When we stumble upon this way of life, it is the best thing ever, and it changes everything. It turns our lives completely upside down.

The kingdom of God is a present way of living that we can choose to be a part of. But it is also a future reality. In other words, it is not always visible to us. We can do the right thing in this moment and still suffer because of it. There is still injustice in the world; there is still misery and pain. But mixed into the messiness of the world are elements of the kingdom of God emerging. This is one of the reasons Jesus compared the kingdom of God to yeast: "The kingdom of heaven is like yeast, which a woman took and hid in a bushel of wheat flour until the yeast had worked its way through all the dough" (Matthew 13:33). Yeast is a leavening agent that converts the sugars in the dough into gases, transforming the taste and texture of the bread.

When we actively "strive first for the kingdom of God" (Matthew 6:33 NRSV), we are pointing to those times and places where God's will is being done and we are able to join into that activity. This is the language of the Godward life. It is a life of partnership with God. When people center their lives on God and celebrate God's action through worship, they begin to reveal the kingdom of God in the world around them.

INSPIRED BY THE PAST

Christianity has a long and rich history of communities of people who lived a Godward, God-centered life. Their communities carry two distinct characteristics: meaningful worship and revealing God's kingdom in the world. These folks saw the reality of the world through the eyes of a loving God, and because of that, they could not go on doing "business as usual." Nor could they keep from praising God.

I've already shared about one such community, that is Iona in Scotland. I encourage you to look into their story more closely. They are not the only ones. As we look at three other communities, I invite you to seek inspiration and insight from their experiences. We are not called to mimic these people; however, we can often draw profound principles from them and their relationship with God.

THE EARLY CHURCH: ACTS 2

As Christians, we are fortunate to have the astonishing Book of Acts to help us understand what a Godward, Spirit-led community can look like. While the book is generally known as the Acts of the Apostles, it could also be called the Acts of the Holy Spirit, as the Spirit weaves throughout the story bringing guidance and power. The early church emerges within this pattern:

- Prayerfully seeking the Spirit's leading (Godward Life)
- Following the Spirit's guidance, moment by moment (Kingdom Living)
- Praising God for what the Spirit has done (Worship)
- Then returning to prayerfully seeking the Spirit's leading (Godward Life)

This was the pattern of their life, and it was the fuel for their worship.

We can see this illustrated from the beginning of the book as Jesus leaves them with the instructions to wait for the Holy Spirit (Acts 1:4-5). The disciples are obedient to this instruction and return to Jerusalem to see what happens. In the second chapter of Acts, the Holy Spirit descends upon those who were gathered together and miraculously gives them the gift of speaking in the languages of Jews who were visiting Jerusalem from distant lands. The scene culminates with Peter's proclamation of who Jesus is and an invitation to change their thinking and their lives, and many believed him.

Near the end of the chapter, we get this snapshot of the early church:

> Every day, they met together in the temple and ate in their homes. They shared food with gladness and simplicity. They praised God and demonstrated God's goodness to everyone. The Lord added daily to the community those who were being saved. (Acts 2:46-47)

Nestled into this passage, easily overlooked is that phrase, "prais[ing] God." The early church has worship at the center of its daily life. It was as common as eating. And their praise is not the result of numerical success. They were worshipping God as a response to the activity of the Holy Spirit.

Active Application: Early Church Living

If we could step into a daily rhythm that is modeled after the early church, what might it look like? Is it possible that each day you could do the following?

- *Seek the Holy Spirit's guidance through prayer, Scripture reading, and discernment (Godward Life).*
- *When you feel nudged by the Holy Spirit, follow that leading (Kingdom Living).*
- *Praise God by telling the story of what God has done (Worship).*

How might such a rhythm impact you? How might such a rhythm impact your community?

BENEDICTINE MONASTERIES

When I was beginning my senior year of high school, my brother, Michael, who is eight years older than me, entered a Benedictine monastery in southern Indiana. It wasn't shocking, exactly, but it did take my family into uncharted territory. For generations, my family had grown up in rural Indiana, attending the nearest United Methodist church. We were proud Methodists, and I remember sitting in Sunday school class and talking about Catholics with an air of judgment and perhaps suspicion: "Are they even Christians?"

When Michael went to college, he went to the University of Dayton, a private, Roman Catholic college. At some point, he converted to Catholicism. No one in the family disowned him, and it seemed to be a life-giving change for him. After college, he was a band director for a few years (my band director, actually—but that's another book), then he took a job working at a nearby Catholic church. In the midst of that work, he felt called to a monastic life and moved to Saint Meinrad's Benedictine Monastery in southern Indiana. Again, it wasn't a shocking move; it fit in the trajectory of his spiritual journey. But it was definitely unfamiliar territory for my family.

We could only visit the monastery periodically. And when we did, it felt like entering another world. Even the drive into the town was striking. One moment, we were driving past small family farms in Indiana, and the next moment, we rounded a hill and there appeared to be a small German village with a beautiful cathedral looming over it. Inside, the monastery was just as otherworldly and fascinating. The grounds were beautifully kept. The monks moved about quietly in flowing black robes. And their days rotated between two pillars: *prayer* and *work* (in Latin, *ora et labora*). I was immediately taken with their lifestyle.

After a few years, my brother left the monastery. As it turns out, the community was made up of human beings with their own struggles and issues, just like every other community. But what I had witnessed when visiting him in that place was a way of living life that stretched back more than 1500 years!

Benedict of Nursia[13]

The Benedictine tradition is the result of one man's work at bringing together the wisdom of Christians who had been stepping out of society for a few hundred years. Benedict was born in the fifth century in what is modern-day Umbria, Italy. He was born of a noble family and was sent to Rome to study. But there, he was disenchanted with life and left the city to find a place more suited to his desires. He settled in a cave outside of Rome where he was able to learn from a monk who lived in a community nearby. Benedict matured in this season and became a person sought after for wisdom. Eventually, he was asked to serve as the head of the monastery that was near to his cave, but it did not go well. He was more ascetic in his practices than the monks preferred, and legend has it that they tried to poison him. He left that monastery, but he appears to have grown from that failure and began founding religious communities afterward. All told, he started twelve communities, and at the end of his life, he wrote a guide for monastic communities which became known as the foundational *The Rule of Saint Benedict*.[14]

The book is a powerful blend of spiritual wisdom and practical advice. He helps communities explore who should be the head of the community and how to structure their life together. It also introduces this powerful idea of work and prayer. Each Benedictine community is autonomous, so their interpretations of the rule may vary. However, there is a general understanding that the monastic life is structured around a pattern of praying multiple times a day in the midst of work, which could include manual labor and study or teaching.

The prayer life of the Benedictine monk is worshipful. It includes the Psalms, which are packed with words of praise and recount what God has done. But again, it is important to see that their worship is not all they do. Instead, their worship lays the foundation of a Godward life as they enter the world to do their work. And that Godward life is still being embodied today by Benedictine Brothers and Sisters.

Benedictines Today

A decade after my brother left Saint Meinrad's monastery, I would find another Benedictine monastery that would show me again how powerful this tradition can be. It was the Benedictine Sisters of Mount St. Scholastica who would train me as a spiritual director. Not only did they train me in spiritual direction, they also revealed how profoundly loving a community can be. Mount St. Scholastica is one of the soul-safest places I have ever visited. It is a truly different place.

Kathleen Norris describes Benedictine monasteries as carrying a deep difference from the world. In pondering this difference and the future of the Benedictine tradition, she shares the insight of one monk:

> The basis of community is not that we have all our personal needs met here, or that we find all our best friends in the monastery. . . . What we have to struggle for, and to preserve, is a shared vision of the *why* . . . why we live together. It's a common meaning, reinforced in the scriptures, a shared vision of the coming reign of God.[15]

"The coming reign of God" is what I witnessed the Sisters pursuing at Mount St. Scholastica. This shared vision of why they live and work together is reinforced throughout their day. Each time they gather for morning, noon-day, and evening worship and prayer, they are turning Godward and inviting the Holy Spirit to speak into their lives individually and as a community. This worship guides them into their work which reaches to a broad range of topics including spiritual formation, education, elder care, creation care, and works focused on social justice. They are a city built on a hill!

Active Application: Benedictine Spirituality

The Benedictine life is often described as a rhythm of work and prayer (which is worshipful). If we could broaden our understanding of prayer to include gratitude, petition, and listening, how might you individually include the rhythm of work and prayer (ora et labora) *into your personal life? Here are a few suggestions:*

Individually

- Set aside a period of time each morning for prayer and praise. You might utilize a prayer book such as *The Book of Common Prayer, An Iona Prayer Book,* or *Common Prayer: A Liturgy for Ordinary Radicals*. Or you may wish to simply have time with God that could include savoring your morning cup of coffee followed by reading a psalm and then talking with God. You could share what is on your heart and then invite God to speak into your life.

- As you move from this prayer time into your day, offer your work to God as an act of co-laboring with God. Offer your gifts, your time, your interests and curiosities to God. Invite God to guide you through your many tasks, whether those tasks are mundane (like washing dishes) or monumental (like making a multimillion-dollar proposal). Ask Jesus how he would do these things. Ask the Spirit to root you in love with every interaction.
- Then throughout your day, allow short periods of thirty seconds to two minutes when you can turn back toward God. These moments could be times of breath prayer, such as "Come, Holy Spirit" or "Jesus, I belong to you." Or they might be short breaks to name what you are grateful for from the day. And they can also include moments of once again inviting God to guide you throughout each decision and action you take during the day. Again, allow this time to root you in God's love.
- At the end of the day, reflect back over the day, asking the Holy Spirit to reveal to you where you did, in fact, co-labor with God. What gifts did you receive from the day? Offer words of thanks for those gifts.

In Community

- In addition to traditional Sunday worship, look for a time once or twice a week when you can join with a small group of folks for prayer and praise. This time could be in the morning, using one of the structured prayer books mentioned previously. It could also be a time of sharing what is unfolding in life and a specific way we need God's help in this moment.

- Community gatherings can also be in the evening around the dinner table, and they can be quite simple. My wife and I gather about once a week with a few friends, and as we share a meal, we often answer the question: What moment from today are you most thankful for? Everyone participates, from the oldest adults to the youngest talking children. While the conversation is rarely somber, it is truly worshipful, generating a heart of gratitude and turning us toward God.

TAIZÉ

Another community that is inspiring and countercultural is the Taizé community of France. Much younger than the Benedictine tradition, the community came into being in the midst of World War II. Brother Roger Schütz felt a longing to live the teachings of Jesus in a daily and concrete way. When Germany took occupation of France, Brother Roger saw his opportunity to provide care for those who were suffering under the oppression of war. He purchased a small abandoned house and outbuildings in the village of Taizé. There, he began offering shelter to refugees of the war. Eventually, the Gestapo suspected something was happening at the house, and Brother Roger along with everyone else in the house had to flee.

Brother Roger fled to Geneva where he lived until the war ended. While in Switzerland, he connected with a few other like-minded men. When the war was over, they all moved back to Taizé and began their work of reconciliation and prayer. Their worship involved simple, meditative singing, combined with Scripture, communion, and periods of silence. To this day, it is a very reflective form of worship that helped them to be grounded in God's love. This would be important for their work of reconciliation.

In post-World War II Europe, reconciliation was difficult work. People were not only recovering from the physical ravages of war, but also the psychological and emotional trauma of living in war-torn areas. In such circumstances, it is difficult to begin the process of rebuilding, reconciling, and enacting justice, but that was the very task at hand. There is a reason we call those who lived through this era the Greatest Generation. Brother Roger and the early Taizé community stepped into this space and began building bridges between groups for reconciliation.

The work of Brother Roger during World War II was heroic. He offered a safe hiding place for refugees and war victims who were escaping German-occupied France. Brother Roger took in anyone who showed up looking for shelter. I suspect that many of us, if we had been living in the village of Taizé at the time, would have been supportive of his efforts. It was the obvious, Christlike action to take.

However, after World War II, Brother Roger and the three other men who formed the Taizé community did something that is much more countercultural: they began visiting German prisoners of war, and "even gained permission from the authorities to invite them as guests to the house for dinner, though food was sparse."[16] Such actions were looked upon with great criticism by the locals. "Anti-German sentiments grew in the area to the extent that some of the local women killed a young German Catholic priest in one of the prisoner-of-war camps located near Taizé."[17]

Let's contextualize the reconciliation work the Taizé community was doing in post WWII. Imagine that after the terrorist attacks in the US on September 11, 2001, those who had perpetrated the attacks, instead of being sent to prison in Guantanamo Bay, were incarcerated in a prison near your home. Can you imagine the anger and hostility that your neighbors (and perhaps you) would have held for these prisoners? It isn't hard to imagine people lining up every day at the walls outside the prison just to taunt and jeer at these prisoners. Now, imagine that a group of men from your town decided they would go every day and enter the prison and pray for and with these prisoners. How would your neighbors have responded to this group of men? How would you have responded to this group of men?

If you can imagine people being suspicious, even hostile, toward that group of men, then you know how people felt about the Taizé community following the Second World War. And yet, we know that Jesus commanded us to love our enemies and to pray for those who persecute us. Most importantly, for our purposes here, we must remember that their acts of reconciliation toward the prisoners of war were sustained by their life of worship of God. Because they lived a Godward life, they were led to respond to the Germans, not as French citizens, but as residents of the kingdom of God.

The work of reconciliation remains the primary identity of the Taizé community. As healing after the war continued, their reconciliation work was more in the form of ecumenism. In *The Sources of Taizé,* Brother Roger writes, "In that unique communion which is the Church, oppositions both ancient and new are tearing the Body of Christ apart. The luminous ecumenical vocation is and always will be a matter of achieving a reconciliation without delay."[18]

Taizé Worship

Taizé worship is one of the most life-giving forms of worship I have ever experienced. At its heart, it is worship that is focused on becoming quiet so we can listen deeply to the heart of God. While it is true that the music is beautiful (and I've been told their worship space is also beautiful), it is really the way Taizé worship leads us to a place of listening that makes it so transformative, because it is in that space of listening that God can give us the words of life that we so desperately need.

Taizé worship might best be described with three words: *simplicity, songs,* and *silence*. These qualities come together in a way that has a gentle but powerful flow to it.

Simplicity

The style of Taizé worship is first of all very simple. There aren't many elements to it. This can be a refreshing change from many worship gatherings that include multiple announcements, starts and stops, and what can sometimes feel like busyness. The simplicity of Taizé worship invites those gathered to be present to the moment, to sink down into the reality of their lives and their relationship with God. If that last sentence makes you uncomfortable, then you have read it correctly. We often fear being quiet before God. We fear that God will look at us with disappointment and loathing. We fear coming face-to-face with our own pain and disappointment with life.

But the gift of Taizé's simple style of worship is that when we are present to God and the moment (even with all our pain and fear), we discover a God who loves us unconditionally and walks beside us in our suffering. Without busyness to distract and numb us, we can experience the healing presence of Christ among us.

Songs

Another key element of Taizé worship is the music. Over the decades, the Taizé community has crafted simple, beautiful songs that often use lyrics based on Scripture or writings from Christians throughout history. Because the songs are short, they can be sung multiple times, and with each pass through the song, the community can engage the moment more fully and listen for how God is speaking to them through the song.

One of my favorite songs is titled, "Nothing Can Trouble," and it is based on a quote from Teresa of Avila.

Nothing can trouble,
nothing can frighten.
Those who seek God shall never go wanting.
Nothing can trouble,
nothing can frighten.
God alone fills us.

That's it! That's the whole song, and that is also the true message of the song, conveyed in simple yet powerful words that are worth repeating over and over again. The more we sing it, the more it sinks down into our soul, shaping the way we live. By grace, we grow into the type of people who are not troubled or frightened because God gives us all we need.

Silence

Finally, there is the silence of Taizé worship. Once again, this is a rare element in the worship services you and I would find at an ordinary church. Typically, on a Sunday morning, if there is silence in worship it means there is a technical difficulty or someone has forgotten to do something. Because of our fear of silence, we tend to avoid it at all costs.

But with Taizé worship, we can enter gently into the silence because of the simple structure, the repetitive songs, and the use of Scripture. There in the silence, we can be present to God. Yes, our mind wanders; yes, there are distractions; yes, we feel uncomfortable, but that isn't all. For it is also in the silence that we meet with the risen Christ who welcomes us as we are, reveals our identity as beloved children, and invites us to love and serve the world.

Active Application: Taizé Worship

- *Find Taizé resources. The Taizé community has created CDs, YouTube videos, and books of worship that give guidance to what I have described.*
- *Find a Taizé worship community. If this style of worship speaks to you, you may be able to find a group of people in your community who gather for Taizé worship on a regular basis. If there is no such group in your community, perhaps you could start one.*
- *Listen for God. Following a model similar to the Taizé community, listen to a recording of a Taizé song, spend time with a short passage of Scripture, and then hold silence as you prayerfully listen for God. This can be a great gift to your journey as you seek to live the Godward life.*

INTO THE WORLD

A Community's Calling

We can hear the stories of communities like the early church, the Iona Abbey, Mount St. Scholastica, and Taizé, and be inspired, but a question remains about our own calling into the world. There might never be a book written or a documentary made about your worshipping community, but that doesn't mean it is insignificant. As the contemporary Christian song, "Dream Small," by Josh Wilson observes:

> *These simple moments change the world . . .*
> *Dream small*

I was fortunate enough to be cousins with the singer/songwriter, Rich Mullins (who wrote "Awesome God" and "Step by Step," to name a few). He also served as a spiritual mentor to me when I was in my late teens and early twenties before his tragic death. He once told me that we all have the same calling, and it isn't hard to figure out what that calling is: we are to love. I found those words to be very freeing. As we move into the world, we don't have to find the one, narrow path of action that God will bless. Instead, we simply must love God and others along the way. Our calling begins to reveal itself as we discover the gifts, curiosities, and passions we possess that help us love God and others.

A very helpful quote from Frederick Buechner points to this idea: "The place God calls you to is the place where your deep gladness and the world's deep hunger meet."[19] For some people, this intersection can be quickly named, but I have found that for most people, it is a slow discovery that becomes clearer only one step at a time. Likewise, for a community of people, the unfolding of our calling can happen even more slowly.

For Brother Roger and the Taizé community, we could broadly say the expression of that love came through reflective worship and reconciliation work in the world. For George MacLeod and the Iona Community, the calling was to love God by working with people the world had cast aside and inviting them into a worshipful community that worked together. For the Benedictine Sisters at Mount St. Scholastica, the calling is to bring together groups of people who live a rhythm of worshipful prayer and work in the world that reveals the coming reign of God's love.

These famous communities and traditions may lead us to believe our calling must be impressive. Instead, we must look at our calling with Kingdom eyes, which do not see as the world sees. Just as Jesus witnessed the woman giving two copper coins to the treasury and proclaimed, "I assure you that this poor widow has put in more than them all. All of them are giving out of their spare change. But she from her hopeless poverty has given everything she had to live on" (Luke 21:3-4), what we "contribute" may not look like a lot, but it is where our giving comes from that matters most.

We may be called to listen to our neighbors. If we do so from a place of love, it is a great gift. We may be called to grow healthy, clean food. If we do so from a place of love, it is a great gift. We may be called to offer respite to caregivers for short periods of time. If we do so from a place of love, it is a great gift. We may be called to advance the safety of certain groups of people. If we do so from a place of love, it is a great gift. We may be called to care for our children and/or spouse. If we do so from a place of love, it is a great gift.

Furthermore, we must step out into the world and live our calling because it is there that we discover God at work. If our worship seems lifeless, the solution is not to bring in better musicians; it is to be more attentive to the Holy Spirit's leading in the world. Because then we have a reason to worship.

CSI "Calling Scene Investigation"[20]

Discovering our calling, both individually and as a community, can be a little like dusting for fingerprints. We need to be attentive to what is around us, and we need to be intentional about looking for God's leading in our life. But the analogy breaks down in this very key point: God is not trying to hide our calling from us.

The evidence of our community's calling begins to emerge as we consider two key ideas:

- First, we know that we are called as followers of Jesus to love God with our whole being and to love our neighbor as ourselves. These are our boundaries.
- Second, we know that Jesus is already at work in a place before we show up. We can see his work, if we look for it. As we see him at work in the world, we have opportunities to invite people into discipleship under Jesus so that they, too, will become salt, light, and leaven in the world.

Then we grow in specific evidence of our community's calling as we consider a few important questions:

- What are we passionate about as a community? When are we energized by our activities? These questions give us a helpful insight into how God has gifted us to live out our calling of loving our neighbors as ourselves.

- What are we not passionate about as a community? When are we drained, lifeless, and unenergized by our activities? Not every community of faith is gifted to do what every other community of faith is gifted to do. What is life-giving for one community will be draining for another. Likewise, what was life-giving for our community at one point in history may be very draining now. Oftentimes in our faith communities, we keep doing things because we always have. And sometimes that's the only reason anyone can name for doing something. But if resources are tight and energy is low, perhaps those things which are done only because they were done fifty years ago need to be released.
- As we begin to notice what our faith community is passionate about and release the activities that are draining for us, we need to ask the critical question which helps us continue to love God and love our neighbor: Where does our deep passion connect with the deep longing of the world? Another way to phrase it would be to ask: How might our faith community be a blessing to God and the world?

I love the story James Bryan Smith tells in his book, *The Good and Beautiful Community,* of a congregation that was growing elderly but wanted to live out their calling to love people. They felt called to offer love and care to college students, even though they doubted they were cool enough to pull it off. They reached out to Smith, who was a college chaplain at the time, and asked for his counsel. He suggested they welcome the students, give them hugs and food, and offer them care during this transitional season of their lives. "Is that all?" they asked. "Don't we need a rock band in worship?" Smith told them he didn't think so, and he was correct. Smith invited the students to visit the church, and the students loved the warm welcome they received there.

What is key to this story is that there was no hidden agenda. This congregation didn't start by asking the question, "How can we get younger members for our church because we're all old and tired of doing this?" (I've actually heard this before in church meetings.) Instead, they were discerning their calling as a congregation, seeking to love God and love others.[21]

Smith offers this powerful insight:

> Communities become others-centered when they are steeped in the narrative of the kingdom of God. They know that their community is an outpost of the kingdom of God, a place where grace is spoken and lived for as long as is needed. The value of a church is not in its longevity but in its love. The success of a church is not in its size but in its service to the people and the community. We are a people founded by a person [Christ] who never established a church or built a building or led a finance campaign to build impressive buildings. Our leader just came and served and then died for the good of others. I suppose that would be a pretty good mission statement for a church, but one I am not likely to

see: "We exist to serve others and then die, just like our Founder."[22]

Finally, it is important to understand that our calling is not a final destination. Our calling flows out of our gifts and our relationship with God. Just as the mystery of the kingdom of God continues to unfold before us, so, too, our calling continues to grow and change. There may be seasons where we continue to live into the same work over and over again, and there may be times when that work evolves and changes rapidly. The good news is that the kingdom of God is at hand, and all along the way we can reach out to God for guidance.

FROM WORSHIP TO WORLD TO WORSHIP TO WORLD

When the church that James Bryan Smith describes honored their calling, they were revealing the kingdom of God among those college students. They were also able to discover God in action, which gave them reason to worship.

When the Holy Spirit descended upon the first disciples and began giving them direction about where to go and what to say, the early church came into being. They were obedient, and time and again the result of their obedience revealed the kingdom of God and led to spontaneous worship.

When Benedict of Nursia recognized that human life flourishes when it involves a balance of worshipful prayer and work, it sparked the creation of monastic communities all around the world. And today in places like Mount St. Scholastica, that rhythm of worship and work is still impacting their community.

When George MacLeod gathered with unemployed shipbuilders and seminary students on a rustic abandoned island, they were living into their calling. And their work helped reveal the nature of the kingdom of God. It gave rise to their worship which reinforced their work.

When Brother Roger and the other monks of Taizé sought to offer a place where people of different backgrounds could gather for prayer and reconciliation, they were living into their gifts and passions. And their work, difficult though it is, helps show us what the kingdom of God is like. At the same time, that very work gives them reason to praise God and listen deeply in worship.

The Holy Spirit is always ready to help us live a beautiful and valuable story. It won't be easy or predictable, but it will be the best possible story we can live. It will be a story we want to tell again and again, and each telling will stir our hearts to worship. How can we not seek that guidance?

GOD IN THE WORLD

One of the beautiful aspects of worship is that it is fueled by grace, therefore it continues to open more and more widely, and perhaps wildly! Not only does our intentional act of worship shape us into people who co-labor with God in the world, it also forms us into people who burst into worship in unexpected places and ways. That is a joyous possibility.

Questions for Personal Reflection and Group Discussion

1. The author begins the chapter by describing a visit to the Iona community in Scotland. Have you ever visited a worshipping community different from your own and been inspired? If so, take time to share that experience. If you have not had that experience, is there a worshipping community you might be able to visit?

2. How does this chapter's explanation of the kingdom of God fit with your own understanding? How is it similar? How is it different?

3. After looking more closely at the early church in the Book of Acts, you were invited to consider what it would look like to embrace their pattern of seeking the Spirit's guidance, then following the Spirit's leading, then praising God for what has happened. What would that look like?

4. Have you been exposed to Benedictine spirituality before? If so, what would you add to the description given in this chapter? What is most intriguing to you about the Benedictine spiritual tradition?

5. How does the description of Taizé worship sound to you? (No judgment here; you may find it terrifying or horrible to be silent.) Why do you feel the way you do about it?

6. Take a few minutes and try to describe the calling of your faith community.

CHAPTER 4

Worship in Unexpected Places

Every year in the town of Winfield, Kansas, there is a bluegrass festival that draws several thousand people. I was introduced to the festival a few years ago, and it is now a mainstay of my annual activities. There is a lot to love about this festival: great musicians (the style of music extends beyond bluegrass into folk, country, and fusions of everything else), eclectic people, and festival camping. Now this last point is important. It isn't camping; it is festival camping. People come in with campers, tents, and homemade contraptions, and we all get packed into the fairgrounds pretty tightly. But festival camping is more than just sleeping closely with others. It is also about jam circles. Many (perhaps most) of the folks who come to the festival bring their instruments, and at any given point throughout the day and night, the sound of guitar, banjo, mandolin, bass guitar, and/or ukulele floats through the air, like campfire smoke. And beautifully, these jam circles are open. So, people take their instruments and move from camp to camp playing with and learning from others.

With this as the backdrop, some friends of mine started Camp Fork-n-Folk. It is a place where breakfast is served every morning, and folk music is played all day long. It is a space that is seeking to draw out our better angels by reflecting on the music that has helped inspire movements for peace, justice, and reconciliation throughout our history. Music by people like Woody Guthrie, Pete Seeger, Malvina Reynolds, and Elizabeth Cotten shape the canon.

One night we were jamming when we came upon the song, "Old Time Religion." It is a traditional spiritual that is fun and simple. I remember singing it during vacation Bible school as a kid. The lyrics are simple:

Give me that old time religion,
Give me that old time religion,
Give me that old time religion,
It's good enough for me!

Then you name other people it was good for . . .
It was good for the Hebrew children,
It was good for the Hebrew children,
It was good for the Hebrew children,
And it's good enough for me!

At Camp Fork-n-Folk, there is an added element. Once a few of the traditional verses have been sung, people can call out the names of people who have been important in their own spiritual journey. Some folks call out the names of people we only know through books and interviews but who have had a profound impact on us, such as Desmond Tutu, Dorothy Day, and John Wesley. Some will call out the names of individuals they know personally. One year, my friend Adam named one of his former youth group members, Sam, who had lost his life. We raised our voices for Sam. Then another friend, Justin, named his grandmother, and we raised our voices with her name. Then another friend, Ashley, lifted up the name of our friend, Mike, who wasn't able to join us this year at the festival, and we raised our voices with his name. And on and on it went.

When the song had ended, there was a glow of gratitude on our faces. We had named something deep in our hearts: gratitude for these people whom God has brought into our lives. With that gratitude was both grief and joy. We had spoken their names into the circle so the community could lift them up in a song of celebration, an offering to God. It was worship—in a jam circle: a place you might not expect to find worship happening. And it could easily have been missed.

DISCIPLES WORSHIP JESUS

Worship does have a way of happening in unexpected places. This is the result of a God who delights in surprising us. So, while we can talk somewhat mechanically about worship as a spiritual practice whereby we respond to what God has done, the joy of worship is better understood as an effervescent energy bubbling out of our souls when we see who God is and what God has done. It comes in those moments when the beauty of the sunset makes you stop and stare with your mouth open. It comes in the tears of joy when much needed help comes to your aid. For the disciples, it came a few times when they saw Jesus do things they didn't think could be done.

In Matthew 14, we hear the story of Jesus walking on water. Peter joins him by walking on the water, and then they climb into the boat. Then we read: "When they got into the boat, the wind settled down. Then those in the boat *worshipped* Jesus and said, 'You must be God's Son!'" (verses 32-33, italics added). This is striking because the journey of the Gospels largely revolves around a question of who Jesus is. There is much questioning and doubt around him being the Messiah because he is not fulfilling the role of the Messiah in ways people expected. And yet, he also walks on water.

There are aspects of this story that I just can't relate to. I have never been on a wind-buffeted boat and seen Jesus walking on the water. But I believe the invitation of the story is to look for areas of our lives that feel like wind-buffeted boats. Have you ever felt stuck in a tumultuous situation in life? Perhaps that situation was your boat. Have you ever experienced God approaching you through that situation in a way that you did not expect? Those moments can be both terrifying ("It is a ghost!") as well as exhilarating ("Lord, if it is you, command me to come to you on the water.").

Whether our shaky little boat is a life-changing experience, like a cancer diagnosis, or a smaller moment, like being in the dentist chair, if we experience God's presence in a way we did not expect that brings peace and assurance, it may lead us to respond as the disciples did: worshipping God!

My Life Flows on in Endless Song

This experience of having God surprise us in the midst of struggle reminds me of the old hymn, "How Can I Keep from Singing?"

1) *My life flows on in endless song;*
above earth's lamentation,
I catch the sweet, though far-off hymn
that hails a new creation.

2) *Through all the tumult and the strife,*
I hear the music ringing.
It finds an echo in my soul.
How can I keep from singing?

"Above earth's lamentation" and "through all the tumult and the strife," the hymn writer is experiencing God's grace in the form of hope. It is the hope of a new creation which echoes in her soul. Such music calls her to sing, and she can't help but to do so.

In the third verse, we see other ways that life can be a painful struggle, and also how God can remain faithful in the midst of that struggle.

3) What though my joys and comfort die?
The Lord my Savior liveth.
What though the darkness gather round?
Songs in the night he giveth.
Refrain) No storm can shake my inmost calm,
while to that Rock I'm clinging.
Since Christ is Lord of heaven and earth,
how can I keep from singing?

There is much loss in this verse. Joys and comforts die, darkness gathers round, storms rage on, but the living Christ remains the security of the hymn writer. Christ meets her, giving her songs to endure the darkness and a refuge to cling to. With gifts as rich as these, she cannot keep from singing.

This is worship in unexpected places. In the places of darkness, doubt, struggle, and suffering, when a far-off hymn comes to our ears, we have the opportunity to join that song.

JESUS' MOMENTS OF PRAISE

As Jesus lived out his calling of proclaiming the kingdom of God, he also revealed a joyful, worshipful posture at various moments. For example, in Luke 10, after the disciples return from a mission of proclaiming the presence of God's kingdom and healing, they return with joyous news. Jesus is moved by what they share and spontaneously offers a worshipful prayer: "I praise you, Father, Lord of heaven and earth, because you've hidden these things from the wise and intelligent and shown them to babies. Indeed, Father, this brings you happiness" (verse 21).

More subtly, there are moments when Jesus is described as being amazed, "filled with wonder."[23] It is a striking image that the Son of God, the Source of All Life, should be filled with wonder at . . . well . . . anything. The Gospel of John describes Jesus as the Word who has been since the beginning of all things, the Word who "was with God and . . . was God. The Word was with God in the beginning. Everything came into being through the Word, and without the Word nothing came into being" (John 1:1-3). Jesus reveals a God who looks with wide eyes at the world, instead of viewing it as yesterday's news. At various times, Jesus shows amazement. To be filled with wonder seems like a fantastic way to describe a Godward life that is bubbling up in worship.

In Matthew 8, Jesus is approached by a Roman centurion who is seeking the healing of his servant who is paralyzed and in terrible distress. This Roman centurion is part of the military that is occupying Israel and is therefore an outsider to the Jewish religious community. Without hesitation, Jesus offers to go to the centurion's house and cure the servant, but the centurion declines this offer, first because he doesn't believe he is worthy to have Jesus in his home, and second because he believes Jesus is powerful enough to heal the servant without going to his house. In verse 10, we read: "When Jesus heard him, he was *amazed* and said to those who followed him, 'Truly I tell you, in no one in Israel have I found such faith'" (Matthew 8:10 NRSV, italics added).

It makes me smile to picture Jesus being amazed at the centurion's faith. Here is Jesus, delighting in this discovery, this treasure. I can easily imagine being there in that moment and having Jesus turn to me after the centurion told Jesus he didn't have to come to his house and Jesus being taken aback, with his mouth a little open for a moment before he says, "Wow! In no one in Israel have I found such faith." I can feel the joy of Jesus in that moment. Because Jesus embodied the Godward life, Jesus' response of amazement is an act of worship. He is worshipping God because the centurion's faith reveals God is breaking through in an unexpected place.

PLACES OF UNEXPECTED WORSHIP

Perhaps worship begins to invade our everyday lives if we are able to be amazed. Whether we are amazed by the depth of sharing around a jam circle, amazed by the beauty of creation, or amazed by the Holy Spirit's work in our neighborhood, it all opens a pathway for calling out to God with gratitude and praise. So, let's look at a few examples of unexpected places where worship can happen in our own lives.

In Creation

Nestled in the Flint Hills of Kansas is a beautiful place called Rock Springs Camp, a 4-H camp that covers seven hundred acres of land. It is remote and has terrible cell service, which are features I value greatly. It is tucked into a valley where a natural spring bubbles to the surface. Because of its size and purpose, the camp has an amazing array of trees, plants, and landscape. As you climb the trails up out of the valley, you arrive at amazing vistas of the open prairie where you can see waving prairie grass for miles.

I am fortunate enough to go to this camp about three times a year to provide spiritual direction for retreatants. Whenever I am here, the words of Hildegard of Bingen ring true: "All of creation is a song of praise to God." From the mysterious shroud of the morning fog, to the diffusion of light through the autumn leaves, to the vastness of stars that can be seen in such a dark place, again and again my attention is captivated and I am turned to a posture of praise to the God who loves us enough to give us places like this. And this is in Kansas—not a state that is known for its beauty, even though it truly is beautiful.

One day as I walked along the path toward the gathering space for retreatants, I found myself walking slower and slower as creation kept surprising me with gifts along the way. It started when I stepped out the door and found myself facing a small field of prairie grass that stands five feet tall. As I walked the perimeter of this field, it waved gently in the breeze revealing hues of green, yellow, and red. And the drying blades of grass scraped against one another producing a percussive rhythm and voice. The percussion of the grass was met with applause by the cottonwood trees that stand along the banks of the creek, clicking their leaves together in a way that echoes the soft babbling of the creek that feeds them. This small stream passes over rocks and curves around the landscape, gently and playfully murmuring. The sights, sounds, smells, and sensations made me feel very close to a God who loves me. I felt I was walking through the hymn, "This Is My Father's World."

This is my Father's world,
He shines in all that's fair;

In the rustling grass I hear Him pass,
He speaks to me ev'rywhere.

With tears in my eyes, I could say nothing but thank you to the God of creation. I was amazed.

Active Application: In Creation

Do you have a place in creation you can go to and experience God's "voice" in ways you can't in the everyday run of life? If you have such a place, take a few minutes to write a paragraph about the beauty of that place. Savor the beauty and wonder of that place and then offer what you have written as a prayer of gratitude to God. You might also consider these questions:

- *What does this place teach you about God?*
- *How does this place make you feel?*
- *How do you care for creation? How does caring for creation fit into your relationship with God?*
- *Are you able to go to this place as often as you would like? If not, what changes would you have to make to return there more often?*

If you don't have a place you like to go, find one! Seek out a local park, or ask a friend or your pastor to recommend a place for you to go and be a part of creation. Even if it's a brief visit, taking a bit of time to experience God in an out-of-the-ordinary way will invigorate your experience of worship.

In the Neighborhood

A few years ago, my wife and I along with a few friends started a nonprofit that is focused on strengthening our neighborhood by encouraging people to be good neighbors. We began our work by knocking on doors and getting to know folks to find out what they enjoyed doing and what they cared about. It was a joyful experience.

We met many wonderful people who had fantastic gifts to share. As we were getting to know people, we did not talk about our faith because we did not want people to feel obligated to be Christian in order to share their gifts in our neighborhood. But a surprising thing happened: many people assumed we were Christians, and some of them expressed an interest in finding a place where they could explore their spiritual curiosity. None of us saw that coming!

Because our nonprofit, which is called The Neighboring Movement,[24] was not designed to be a church, we weren't sure what to do at first. We decided to have a monthly potluck and invite people to come together to share what was on their hearts and what they were searching for spiritually. Our small gatherings have included collage making, puzzle assembly, folk singing, and storytelling. We started calling them "Inspiration Nights" because it was so life-giving to hear people share.

One of my favorite nights happened when the group met at my house. We had a few new people, so we had to cram about fifteen people into our living room around folding tables and chairs. People were enjoying their conversations with their neighbors so much, I had to interrupt them to begin our evening discussion. And even then, the group took on a will of its own and people began sharing their own stories of where they were feeling thankful and where they were feeling drained. Some people told jokes, other people shared concerns, and the youngest member of the group, a five-year-old named Prescott, shared a book he had written and illustrated.

We were amazed!

Active Application: In the Neighborhood

Do you have a community of people with whom you connect who live in your area? This could be a community group or even just a gathering of friends. The next time you gather with this group, think about the aspects of this gathering that are worshipful—how God can be praised for the connections and relationships that develop. If you do not have connections with other members of your community, seek some out and join or begin a community fellowship with a group of friends.

In the Workplace

When I was thirteen years old, I had the good fortune to begin working as a free farmhand on my neighbor's family farm. Bill and Melba McClure and their four children were the picture of American farming as it used to exist. The small family farm raised everything: dairy, pork, chickens, eggs, soybeans, corn, wheat, oats, and hay. Melba was born and raised in New Orleans and talked and worked faster than anyone I had ever met in my life. She and Bill had met in the Navy. Bill had grown up in Indiana and together, he and Melba had set up life on these one-hundred-plus acres of land.

Bill was the quintessential farmer. He could do all manner of craftsmanship from auto mechanic to welder to weatherman to biologist to veterinarian to heavy equipment operator. But what struck me most about Bill was that he was not religious (I don't know that he ever went to church), *and* he was spiritual. He was a quiet man. We could work all day with only a few words passing between us. But in his quiet way, he seemed to be in harmony with the land. He understood the unromantic nature of farming, the frailty of crops and livestock, the extreme hours of work, and the impossibility of a day off for a dairy farmer. And yet, he also knew the joy of co-laboring with creation to bring life, nutrition, and beauty into the world. Though he spoke very rarely, when he did, it was often to tell a joke followed by a quick smile.

From Bill, I learned that work is sacred and worshipful. It is not just something we do to make money. It is meant to resonate with our souls and connect with the world, even when it is difficult. Worshipful work allows moments of awe to break in, like magic. Sometimes that magic comes in small moments, like the time Bill brought an armful of sweet corn in from the field for us to eat. There is nothing more delicious than sweet corn fresh from the field that you have helped grow. We savored every bite and glowed with joy.

Other times, worshipful work is magical in life-altering ways, borne out of struggle and survival. One day in the midst of our regular chores, we realized one of the heifers was calving in the field and was having difficulty. We went quickly to the field and began deliberating what needed to be done. Bill feared the calf would not pass, and both the calf and the mother would be lost. Reaching into the birth canal, Bill was able to take hold of one of the calf's hooves. Once the hoof was visible, we tied twine around the hoof and began pulling to assist the heifer in the birthing process. One of the daughters and I were on one end of the twine with the calf on the other, while Bill and Melba comforted and coaxed the heifer. After much struggle, the calf came free. I had never seen anything like that in my life.

We were all amazed.

And they named the calf after me!

Active Application: In the Workplace

My years of working on the McClures' farm is a bundle of sacred moments. And while time has eroded some of my sense of wonder, I find the roots I put down on that farm still sustain me. Nevertheless, I also find that of all the places where worship can happen, work may be the most difficult. Whether we work in the home, in the office, on the farm, or a multiplicity of jobs, it is difficult to remain present to the sacred unfolding in our work.

How might you give thanks and praise to God in the midst of the tasks of your day? Perhaps you could count small victories and give thanks for those. Perhaps you could look back over the many years you have done your job to search out ways God has been active in your endeavors. Perhaps there is an invitation for you to be more deliberate and attentive in your work to notice the subtle beauty of what you do. Perhaps you need pauses for jokes and joy in the midst of (and about) your work.

In Small Groups

I tend to imagine worship happening in two different settings:

- The safe worshipping community of one hundred people or more. Our voices don't stand out, things are usually planned ahead of time, and regardless of our mood, worship can happen.
- The safety of worshipping alone. No one is present to hear my voice crack, my tummy rumble, or my sorrow or anger.

But there is another setting where worship can and should happen—the small group. Worship in small groups can be a powerful and life-giving experience. However, it can also feel vulnerable and scary.

About a decade ago, Catherine and I began meeting once a week for morning prayer with two other friends. Over the years, our group has fluctuated as people have joined and left for various reasons. Because we meet in the morning, we don't always have much time to visit. We are all a little sleepy when we gather, but we share coffee and check-in and then begin our time of worship together. For most of these years, we have used the book, *Common Prayer:*

A Liturgy for Ordinary Radicals by Shane Claiborne, Jonathan Wilson-Hartgrove, and Enuma Okoro. We share leadership using a rotation model, so someone different leads each week. We can each do as much or as little preparation as we want to do. We usually sing one or two songs from a big binder of songs we've gathered over the years.

Each one of us has had to find our own way of leading. There are surprising questions that arise when you are leading a small group of folks for the first time. For example, how will you lead into the Lord's Prayer? You could just jump right in with the words "Our Father who art in heaven," or you could give a lead-in line such as "Now, let us join our voices in the prayer Jesus taught us." How much silence will you allow during the prayer time before you move on? What song or songs will you choose and why?

We've also learned how to be in the room together and offer each other grace. When a song goes poorly, we chuckle about it. When a person loses their place, the person next to them offers a hand. When life is difficult, we offer hugs and tissues. When someone's birthday rolls around, we offer fruit and donuts.

This small-group gathering impacts me on many levels. It gives us a chance to turn our attention back toward God at the midpoint of the week. This mid-week adjustment makes the Godward life more natural. The gathering also gives us a small community to connect with on a regular basis. As time allows, we have chances to give each other updates on life and work and worries. This time of sharing life as well as joining together in prayer gives us an emotional and spiritual grounding that is invaluable. And, as mentioned, the model of shared leadership gives us a chance to see what it is like to lead a group of people in prayer, song, and reading. I have found this experience to make me more forgiving of people leading worship in churches because I better understand some of the challenges they face.

Jesus' words of assurance ring profoundly true for our group: "For where two or three are gathered in my name, I am there among them" (Matthew 18:20 NRSV). When we gather together with a small group of folks, it can be a little scary (especially at first), but Christ meets us there and that is amazing!

Active Application: In Small Groups

- *Do you have a small group of friends that you could meet with on a regular basis for Scripture reading, prayer, storytelling, and perhaps singing?*
- *How might you experiment by meeting for a season, such as Advent, Lent, or during the summer, to see how it goes? Give yourself permission to start and stop and make changes as you go.*
- *Where could you meet that would be simple and convenient for most of the group?*
- *What liturgy might you use? There is an order of service in* The United Methodist Hymnal, *and there are other liturgies such as* The Book of Common Prayer, Common Prayer: A Liturgy for Ordinary Radicals, *and* Iona Abbey Worship Book, *just to name a few. And you can certainly create your own liturgy.*
- *If you start worshipping with a small group of people, reflect periodically as a group and individually on how this gathering is impacting your relationship with God and your overall experience of worship.*

. . . *in Worship!*

Pastor Amy Lippoldt was making a presentation to a group of fifteen pastors who were in the final steps of being ordained in The United Methodist Church. She began by asking everyone to take a few minutes to share their name, where they are currently serving, and one way they saw God at work in their previous worship service.

One by one, people began to share. Some stories were fun: like the pastor who started his sermon with a knock-knock joke that made everyone laugh ("Knock, knock!" "Who's there?" "Ach!" "Ach who?" "God bless you!") to the more poignant, like the pastor who got to share in her first immersion baptism, and another pastor who baptized a one-year-old baby born with severe health issues—miraculously alive today.

As each pastor shared, the warmth of the room grew. We were each hearing the stories of how God can and does show up when we gather for worship. I sensed that a few of the pastors hadn't thought about that particular moment until they were asked to reflect. They gained insight and found strength in hearing one another's stories.

Their stories reminded me that sometimes God moves in worship, and that should prompt us to greater worship. Those moments when healing happens, freedom is discovered, and forgiveness is embraced are moments when we can respond to God with even greater joy. We can call out, like the psalmist in Psalm 84:1-4:

> How lovely is your dwelling place,
>   LORD of heavenly forces!
> My very being longs, even yearns,
>   for the LORD's courtyards.
> My heart and my body
>   will rejoice out loud to the living God!
>
> Yes, the sparrow too has found a home there;
>   the swallow has found herself a nest
>   where she can lay her young beside your
> altars,

LORD of heavenly forces, my king, my God!
Those who live in your house are truly happy;
they praise you constantly.

The psalmist does a beautiful job of giving words to our emotions and images in our mind of the result of a worshipful life. It is a life of provision and care. It is a life of abundance. It is a life of joy!

Active Application: In Worship
Answer Amy's question: What is one way you saw God at work in the most recent worship service you attended?

JOY AS A RESULT

Joy Versus Happiness

It has been helpful to me to differentiate between joy and happiness. This is a difference I have constructed; it is not accurate in the actual terms, as the two are technically considered synonyms for one another. Merriam-Webster defines joy as "a state of *happiness* or felicity."[25] They define happiness as "a state of well-being and contentment: *JOY*"[26] (both italics added). Nevertheless, I suspect that the American pursuit of happiness has left us in a position where we need to look for something deeper than happiness.

I consider happiness to be a temporary pleasure. When I eat chocolate, it makes me happy. When I hear a good joke, it makes me happy. Happiness is not bad, but it is determined by external factors, making it temporary. For just as chocolate can make me happy, if I go to eat a piece of bread and discover it is moldy, I will be sad. If someone tells me of an old friend who has passed away, I will be sad.

Joy, on the other hand, is rooted in something deeper than these externals. I have come to believe joy is rooted in God's love for us, God's action in our lives, and God's care. This means that the external sources of my happiness will come and go, along with my happiness, but my joy will remain. This joy is rooted in my identity which is Christ within me. I find proof of my interpretation of this difference in that joy is listed as a fruit of the Holy Spirit (Galatians 5:22-23). Its presence on that list means we don't generate joy; it results from our journey with the Holy Spirit. If we, as branches, remain connected to the vine, who is Christ, the natural fruits will be joy (John 15:1-11).

Francis of Assisi: Perfect Joy

I love the story of a time Francis of Assisi taught, in a parable-like way, about perfect joy. Brother Francis was traveling with his assistant, Brother Leo. It was in the winter, and they were traveling by foot through snow and rain. Over the course of a few miles, Francis would periodically call out to Leo and describe to him amazing things the Franciscan Brothers could accomplish. He would give a few examples, such as "make the lame to walk; make straight the crooked; chase away demons; give sight to the blind, hearing to the deaf, speech to the dumb; and, what is even a far greater work, if they should raise the dead after four days." But then he shocks us with this statement: "Write that this, Brother Leo, would not be perfect joy."

In the story, this happens multiple times. Francis describes amazing activities that the Brothers could accomplish, but each time he tells Brother Leo that this would not be perfect joy.

Finally, Brother Leo poses the question that so desperately needs to be raised: Where is perfect joy? Then Francis answers with a rather shocking story. He tells Leo to imagine that at the end of their lengthy walk, they arrived at the convent and upon arriving, they were hungry, tired, and cold. After knocking on the door, the porter answered, but refused to believe that they were who they said they were. Instead, he kept the door barred and forced them to stay outside in the cold and wet. And if Leo and Francis were able to receive such rejection and hardship with patience, that would be perfect joy. Francis gives these words of wisdom to Brother Leo (and us): "Above all the graces and all the gifts of the Holy Spirit which Christ grants to his friends is the grace of overcoming oneself."[27]

Now, I grant that what the suffering Francis describes in his story is excessive. But I don't think we should allow that to keep us from putting ourselves in the same position. What captures my imagination is the idea of walking with Francis through some task in my own life and having him do the same exercise with me. He would be pulling my focus away from the illusion of happiness and toward the joy of living the Godward life.

Here is an example of what I mean. Each spring semester, I teach a course at nearby Friends University on the connection between Christian spiritual formation and community. So, I imagine Francis sitting with me as I am organizing the syllabus and deciding what books the students will read. Then Francis begins to call to me, just as he did to Brother Leo: "If your teaching were so clear and helpful that every class was a life-changing experience for the students, and you were able to illuminate subjects that had been enigmatic for centuries, write that *this* would not be perfect joy. Or if your students were so inspired by your class that they went out into the world to eradicate poverty, provide clean water to all humanity, and master sustainable living strategies, write, O Matthew, that *this* would not be perfect joy."

At which point, I, much vexed in mind, might respond, "O Francis, then do tell me, where is perfect joy?"

To which he might respond by saying, "Imagine that we arrived at the first day of class and found students you have taught in previous years gathered in protest that you were teaching, that students refused to listen to your lecture or read your assigned text. Imagine that partway through the first class, the president of the university arrived to publicly describe your inadequacies as a professor in front of your students. And as all this was happening, we were able to receive it patiently and view each person with God's love in our heart. Write down, O Brother Matthew, that here, finally, is perfect joy!"

I know this sounds crazy, but it inspires me because it is a snapshot of the life I want to live. I long to discover a life that patiently welcomes all moments, regardless of the circumstances, and remains rooted in the love of God. Worship that is rooted in God's loving action can help us foster this type of life.

I am a long way from this life, but I have also discovered the reality of these ideas. A few years ago, I was living through a season of vocational insecurity. The nonprofit that we started was living up to its category (not-for-profit), and it looked like I would need to find employment someplace else. My fear was that I couldn't get a "real" job because the skills I had developed over the years are not stamped with a certificate or diploma by any institution. I had many sleepless nights as I pondered the death of our efforts in the organization we had created and my lack of marketable skills. As I laid awake at night, all I could do was keep turning to God, asking for help and guidance. I had to let go of the markers of success that I had believed would lead to happiness. And instead, I offered to God a willingness to do whatever needed to be done. And although it took several months, what I discovered was a joy that was free of both my job and my skills. I could be joyful in my work because God had called me to it, and I could be joyful about my skill set because God had given it to me. It didn't matter who certified it.

Eventually, we were able to get the nonprofit to a slightly more stable place, and I even got a part-time job with another organization that valued the skills I brought to the table. But I hold these things lightly for they are not the source of my joy. My joy comes in knowing that my identity in Christ cannot be shaken or lost.

Hebrews 12

The writer of Hebrews gives a description of this rootedness that baffled me for many years, but now I am beginning to understand it. In Hebrews 12, the author describes the earth being shaken and all created things being removed. That removal is the loss of the manufactured identity we build around temporary things like our work, our accomplishments, and our possessions. At some point in our lives, we will all experience the loss of these things. But we are people of hope and joy, and in verses 28-29 we learn why: "Therefore, since we are receiving a kingdom that can't be shaken, let's continue to express our gratitude. With this gratitude, let's serve in a way that is pleasing to God with respect and awe, because our God really is a consuming fire."

God is a consuming fire. But that fire is not fueled by animosity toward us; it is fueled by the loving desire to give us something much larger: life in the kingdom of God. The only way we can receive this gift is to "throw off any extra baggage, get rid of the sin that trips us up, and fix our eyes on Jesus, faith's pioneer and perfecter. He endured the cross, ignoring the shame, for the sake of the joy that was laid out in front of him, and sat down at the right side of God's throne" (verses 1-2).

Christ was moved by joy to endure the suffering and shame of the cross, and we are called to do the same. That which has felt shameful in our lives is actually the space where God's grace can move most powerfully, revealing how deeply we are loved. Once again, we see the wonder of God's action, and how can we keep from singing? How can we keep from responding with joy? How can we keep from being amazed?

JOURNEY TO JOY

The Spirituals

The journey to a life of joy is marked along the way with worship. On a regular basis, and the more often the better, if we can pause to reflect on what God is doing, where God is working, and take a moment to respond to that action with praise, we will be fostering a life of joy.

And please hear me when I say this is not a glib process. I am not inviting you to ignore the areas of suffering and struggle in life. Those areas are real, and the invitation is to allow God to work through those struggles to make them transformative. We see this powerfully incarnated in the lives of those who were enslaved and oppressed through slavery and racism in the US and who expressed their struggle and hope through the singing of spirituals. The spirituals teach us that even in struggle, if we can turn our longing toward God in worship, the Spirit of God will transform us. In a powerful interview with Krista Tippett, Joe Carter describes the transforming power of the spirituals:

> . . . they [the spirituals] were the expression of the great pain and the sorrow. But at the same time, they were always looking upward. They were always reaching. There was always some level of hope, as opposed to the concept of the blues. The blues was just singing about your troubles, and there was no hope. But there's always the glory hallelujah someplace saying, "Oh, and on that glory hallelujah, then we fly." So in the midst of the night, we can fly away to freedom while we're singing these songs.[28]

This is a very poignant differentiation between the spirituals and the blues, and likewise between Christ-centered worship and self-centered worship. The spirituals (and Christ-centered worship) do not deny the pain and sorrow. In fact, the story of Christ's suffering and death, along with many other aspects of the Gospels, gives us permission to express the pain we are feeling. We don't experience healing unless we are given space to express the pain. But it doesn't stop there, because with Christ-centered worship, we are then able to express the hope. James Bryan Smith gives this helpful definition of hope: "certainty in a good future." We may not see this good future in our own lifetime, but we know it is coming. As Christians, we know how the story ends: God's love prevails.

This is worship! Raising our voice in song, even if most of the song needs to be about the pain, we still hold on to the refrain of hope.

> *Nobody knows the trouble I've seen.*
> *Nobody knows, but Jesus.*
> *Nobody knows the trouble I've seen.*
> *Glory, hallelujah!*

This act of worship is transformative. It turns suffering into fuel that burns away all the trappings of our egos and invites us into the larger world of God's kingdom. Carter describes the way this transformation was embodied among slaves. In the same interview, he continues,

> . . . I think that the sorrow became the entrance, the open door, into a whole new world of experience. The slaves could not experience the normal world. They couldn't go out and go shopping. They couldn't buy a house. They couldn't do all the things that the normal white person did. They were slaves, you know? They were whipped, and they had chains. And they found a secret door to take them into that world where the tears are wiped away. And the thing that we find is that in the midst of all of the most horrible pain, some of these powerful individuals lived transcendent, shining lives. They were able to rise up above. They were able to be loving and forgiving in the midst of it all.[29]

"Transcendent, shining lives"; that is the invitation of the worshipful life. It is a life fueled by God's action, and in that relationship, we can then become people who take responsibility for our world!

Rooted in Love

Perhaps it isn't surprising that those who have suffered greatly are able to live transformed lives. I know many who look back on seasons of struggle and see how they drew closer to God. But suffering is not the only path to a life of joy. Richard Rohr points out that both great suffering and great love will move us deeper into a relationship with God.[30] And God's great love for us is present, even in the most mundane of moments.

When we move through our everyday routines, we can do so from a place of love. It can begin with God's love for us—taking a few minutes to realize that every morning God delights to meet us and be with us. God's love for us is not cold or abstract; it is warm and filled with emotion. And when God's love is at the center of our lives, everything can become an act of worship. Love is our center, and joy is our circumference.

For the last couple of years, I have found myself returning again and again to Paul's prayer for the church in Ephesus. The prayer is offered at the end of the third chapter of Ephesians, and it serves as a poetic call to discover a life of worship and joy by discovering a life of love.

> This is why I kneel before the Father. Every ethnic group in heaven or on earth is recognized by him. I ask that he will strengthen you in your inner selves from the riches of his glory through the Spirit. I ask that Christ will live in your hearts through faith. As a result of having strong roots in love, I ask that

> you'll have the power to grasp love's width and length, height and depth, together with all believers. I ask that you'll know the love of Christ that is beyond knowledge so that you will be filled entirely with the fullness of God. (Ephesians 3:14-19)

I know this passage, like most of Paul's writing, can be wordy and difficult to track. First of all, this is a prayer. Paul offers this prayer for the Ephesians, but I believe it is still being offered for you and I.

Notice the language of abundance. There are no boundaries to God's adoptive love, but instead "*every* ethnic group in heaven or on earth" (italics added) can take their name from God. Likewise, Paul describes the riches of God's glory. There is no scarcity here.

The phrase, "that he will strengthen you in your inner selves," calls to my mind the true self that is anchored in the reality of God's love for us. This strength allows us to face any circumstance with confidence that we do not stand alone, but that God stands with us. And this is not an arrogant confidence; it is a gift of the Holy Spirit. Then, in a phrase that looks like parallelism, Paul rephrases the "inner selves" to our "hearts" in the next verse. And it is there in our hearts that the resurrected Christ resides. When we face our inner critics, we do not face them alone, but Christ is there to speak the truth: we are God's children. It means that no matter what swirls around us, we can be rooted and grounded in love.

Rooted. Like an old tree that draws its nutrients and stability from the earth, we are invited to be rooted in God's love. Whenever doubts or fears or troubles or apathy assail us, we can lean into God's love. The result is a life so rooted that it becomes the transcendent, shining life that Joe Carter described.

Grounded. While I doubt that Paul was thinking of electronics when he wrote this word, I think the wisdom here is important for us. To be grounded is to honor our limitations, to acknowledge that we are not the primary character in our own story, but instead it is the divine Trinity. Our lives may be amazing, marvelous stories, but if we remain grounded in love, we are able to name that most of what we have is a gift we have been given.

"That you'll have the power to grasp love's width and length, height and depth, together with all believers . . ." God's love is so astonishing, we need to be well-rooted and grounded to grasp it. We also need to stand in the company of others to really experience it. I take the word *saints* to be both those who have gone before us as well as those who travel with us now. And I am thankful for both. I think of the saints throughout history who have left behind amazing writings that help us make sense of our lives today. Saints like the desert mothers and fathers, the famous Christians of history like Francis and Clare, Benedict and Scholastica, and Mother Teresa and Desmond Tutu. The saints also include my own family tree, those who sought to live faithfully as best as they understood it and handed down to me what I have today.

And the saints are also those who stand with us today. When we gather with others for worship, we get to be all together in a room. So often we forget what a powerful and beautiful gift this is. Yes, it is messy; yes, we all have flaws that rub against each other; but nevertheless, we cannot do this alone.

Then Paul gives us this short but stunning statement, that we might comprehend "the width and length, height and depth" of God's love. This phrase brings to my mind experiences of being at the base of a mountain or on the shore of the ocean. To gaze at something that is so immense makes me feel tiny. It also makes me think of the cosmos, stretching in every direction and including everything. But unlike the ocean and the cosmos which can be cold and life-threatening, the love of God is always, only, ever seeking our good.

And then we read, "that you'll know the love of Christ that is beyond knowledge so that you will be filled entirely with the fullness of God." I love the play on words in that first phrase, "*know* the love of Christ" even though that love is "beyond *knowledge*" (emphasis mine). This type of knowing is not something that can be held in our head; it is all-consuming. It is to know in the same way that we know the love of our spouse or of a child or of a parent or of a friend with every aspect of our being. The result of this knowing is shocking, "that you will be filled entirely with the fullness of God." Wait a minute, the same God whose love extends to every end of the cosmos is now inhabiting my being? And your being? Yes! Words and head-knowledge cannot express this reality. We can only live into it moment by moment, day by day, as we respond with worship and experience joy.

SENDING FORTH

Just like Paul, I am holding you in prayer. I am praying that my words will serve as a gift to you on your journey into the present kingdom of God, into the Godward life of worship and joy. It seems like a lot to ask, but God seems to desire such a discovery.

It seems that God desires to have a deeper, more vibrant relationship than we already have. It is hard to imagine.

In her chapter on worship, Kathleen Norris writes,

> I wanted worship with room for the Holy Spirit, worship hospitable enough to welcome a confused soul such as myself. And there, among strangers, I found it: living worship, slightly out of control, and not terribly educational. Orthodox in the ancient sense, as "right worship," joyful enough to briefly house a living God.[31]

". . . joyful enough to briefly house a living God." That sounds like a miracle to me, and yet it is a miracle I have witnessed again and again. Is it too much to ask? Absolutely not, because we worship a God who has very much proven a desire to draw near to us. Jesus took on flesh and blood "and moved into the neighborhood" (John 1:14 *The Message*), and things haven't been the same since. So, instead of holding back, let us hold each other in the concluding words of Paul's prayer in Ephesians 3:20-21 (CEB):

> Glory to God, who is able to do far beyond all that we could ask or imagine by his power at work within us; glory to him in the church and in Christ Jesus for all generations, forever and always. Amen.

Questions for Personal Reflection and Group Discussion

1. Can you recount a time you have experienced worship in an unexpected place? If so, what happened? What was it like? And how did it impact you?

2. How does it make you feel to picture Jesus' amazement as an act of worship?

3. What is your favorite line from the hymn, "How Can I Keep from Singing"? Why?

4. Do you have a favorite place in creation where you like to connect with God? If so, describe it.

5. How might God be at work in your neighborhood, town, or community?

6. What might "worshipful work" mean for you? How could you pursue it more fully?

7. How would you describe the difference between joy and happiness, according to the author?

8. What was your reaction to Francis of Assisi's explanation of perfect joy?

9. Spend a few minutes reading aloud Ephesians 3:14-21. What catches your attention? What might God be inviting you to receive from this passage?

NOTES

CHAPTER ONE

1 Richard J. Foster, *Celebration of Discipline: The Path to Spiritual Growth* (HarperOne, 1978), 171.

2 Online Etymology Dictionary, *etymonline.com/word/audience* (July 14, 2018).

3 *The Book of Discipline of The United Methodist Church* 2012 (The United Methodist Publishing House, Nashville, 2012), 102.

4 For a more in-depth exploration of the prayer of examen, I highly recommend *Sleeping With Bread: Holding What Gives You Life,* by Dennis Linn, Sheila Fabricant Linn, and Matthew Linn (Paulist Press, 1995).

CHAPTER TWO

5 Here I am, working with material developed by my mentor and colleague, James Bryan Smith. His books, *The Good and Beautiful God, The Good and Beautiful Life,* and *The Good and Beautiful Community* are a powerful exploration of how relationships, stories, and activities shape us. I have modified the language from his original: narratives, practices, and community.

6 CBS News, "Cutting Through Advertising Clutter," by Caitlin Johnson, September 17, 2006, https://www.cbsnews.com/news/cutting-through-advertising-clutter/

7 *Cambridge Dictionary Online,* https://dictionary.cambridge.org/us/dictionary/english/reconciliation

CHAPTER THREE

8 Liturgy is the way the worship is structured and the written prayers that are often said together. They include things like the call to worship, prayers of confession, and Communion preparation.

9 Iona Community website, https://iona.org.uk/about-us/history/; Boston University School of Theology Center for Practical Theology, *Chasing the Wild Goose: The Story of the Iona Community* by Ronald Ferguson, book review by Josh Sweeden, http://www.bu.edu/cpt/resources/book-reviews/chasing-the-wild-goose-the-story-of-the-iona-community/

10 *Iona Abbey Worship Book* (Wild Goose Publications, Glasgow, 2017), 94–95.

11 Pierre Teilhard de Chardin, *Christianity and Evolution,* translated by René Hague (Harcourt Inc., 1969), 92–93.

12 First Corinthians 13:4-8a describes love, and since God is love, we can draw a correlation between the two.

13 Much of this biographical material is drawn from Kathleen Norris's beautifully written book on Benedictine spirituality entitled, *The Cloister Walk* (Riverhead Books, New York, 1997).

14 Encyclopaedia Britannica Online, "St. Benedict" by Michael David Knowles, last updated January 4, 2019, https://www.britannica.com/biography/Saint-Benedict-of-Nursia

15 Kathleen Norris, *The Cloister Walk* (Riverhead Books, New York, 1997), 22.

16 Jason Brian Santos, *A Community Called Taizé* (InterVarsity Press, 2008), 61.

17 Santos, 61.

18 Brother Roger of Taizé, *The Sources of Taizé* (GIA Publications Inc., Chicago, 2000), 27.

19 Frederick Buechner, *Beyond Words: Daily Readings in the ABC's of Faith* (HarperCollins, New York, 2004), 405.

20 Information in this section is from Neighboring Movement.org by SoCe Life, "The Good Neighbor Experiment Lab 4: Re-Cycle," www.NeighboringMovement.org/store

21 James Bryan Smith, *The Good and Beautiful Community* (InterVarsity Press, 2010), 69–70.

22 Smith, 72–73.

CHAPTER FOUR

23 Merriam-Webster Dictionary Online, https://www.merriam-webster.com/dictionary/amaze

24 www.NeighboringMovement.org

25 *Merriam-Webster Dictionary Online,* https://www.merriam-webster.com/dictionary/joy

26 *Merriam-Webster Dictionary Online,* https://www.merriam-webster.com/dictionary/happiness

27 I have paraphrased this story from the website, Missa (www.missa.org), http://www.missa.org/joie_parfaite_e.php

28 *On Being with Krista Tippett,* "Joe Carter: The Spirituals," original air date: May 9, 2003; last updated: August 9, 2018, https://onbeing.org/programs/joe-carter-the-spirituals-aug2018/

29 *On Being with Krista Tippett,* "Joe Carter: The Spirituals."

30 Fr. Richard Rohr OFM, *CAC Foundation Set (DVD): Gospel Call for Compassionate Action (Bias from the Bottom) and Contemplative Prayer.*

31 Kathleen Norris, *Amazing Grace: A Vocabulary of Faith* (Riverhead Books, New York, 1998), 250.

www.ingramcontent.com/pod-product-compliance
Lightning Source LLC
Jackson TN
JSHW030727260226
98476JS00018B/117
9781501877582